The Numerical Structure of Scripture

The Numerical Structure of Scripture

F. W. Grant

LOIZEAUX BROTHERS
Neptune, New Jersey

FIRST EDITION, OCTOBER 1887
TWELFTH PRINTING, OCTOBER 1989

ISBN 0-87213-269-2

PRINTED IN THE UNITED STATES OF AMERICA

PREFATORY NOTE

TO THE REVISED EDITION

A NEW edition of this little volume being called for, it is pleasant to find that in the twelve years that have elapsed since the first was published, so little correction should be needed, when so much further work has been done in regard to the numerals and their application to the structure of Scripture. I have not attempted to do more than make whatever might be called for in this way. The four volumes of the Numerical Bible already published will naturally show development in various ways; but there has been no attempt to develop this correspondingly. In the nature of the book it is but an introduction, for which purpose much enlargement would rather injure it than otherwise.

May the Lord be pleased still to use it for the help of students of the inspired Word.

F. W. GRANT.

Plainfield, N. J. Sept. 25th, 1899.

THE NUMERICAL STRUCTURE

OF

𝔖𝔠𝔯𝔦𝔭𝔱𝔲𝔯𝔢

A SEAL UPON ITS PERFECT INSPIRATION, AND A
DIVINELY GIVEN HELP TO ITS RIGHT
INTERPRETATION

LECTURE I

INTRODUCTORY

I THINK, beloved friends, the best way in which I
can introduce the subject which is to be before us,
will be by stating how the Lord has led me into
the apprehension of it.

The first thing for us, however, is to realize, what I
trust we do, that the Word of God is absolutely that
from beginning to end of it,—every line, I may say,
and letter of it. Of course I do not mean by that at
all that translations do not fail. I do not mean that
that there are not errors of transcription in copies
which have been transmitted to us from old time. But
I do mean that when we get fairly and fully what was
written at first, we have there, absolutely and fully, the
word of God; although He has spoken through man,
and the diverse character of His instruments be appar
ent on every page, yet we have none the less on this
account God's word in unclouded majesty—pure truth,
without any mixture of defect whatever.

And, beloved, while it is a little volume—this Bible

of ours, and thank God it is, so that we can hold it in our hands and carry it in our pockets, yet how large, how immense a book it nevertheless is! Always yielding new fruit to the patient and diligent explorer; age after age does not exhaust it, but continually beckons into fields which lie beyond. If I should say to you that here, in the nineteenth century of the complete revelation, after so many centuries of learned, continuous, believing investigation, there was yet a character of it written upon every page, and of a most important kind, which had wholly escaped research, would it not seem impossible? And yet that is what I do say, and hope to prove to your complete satisfaction before these lectures close,—a character which is itself a most convincing proof of its inspiration in every part, and which offers itself as a key, divinely given to its intelligent apprehension.

Have we still a use for such a thing? Indeed, indeed we have. Of the real meaning of how much of Scripture are we still profoundly ignorant! I might mention whole books—especially of the Old Testament,—of which we know really very little yet. And if you say, We know enough, would it not be to put dishonor upon the large bounty of God, who has given us in all this out of His very heart, not mere intellectual furnishings, but His whole mind in Christ, that we may have fellowship with Him?—a fellowship in which all sanctification lies. "*All* Scripture is given by inspiration of God, and is profitable for doctrine, for reproof, for correction, for instruction in righteousness, that the man of God may be perfect, throughly furnished unto all good works."

Alas! beloved brethren, is it not true that we little believe in the necessity of the *whole* Word for sanctification? Why has God given it as He has, sending His inspired servants one after another, to make it over to us? Has He done more than necessary? Shall we tell Him so? and that we can afford to let a large part of it be practically without use? I feel that what we want first of all to realize is that this blessed Word, being God's word, is worthy of our fullest, deepest attention in every particular. It is in the practical faith of this only that we can expect to find what is in it. We have to *believe* that something is there, in order to find that it is indeed there. In the gospel, of course, God meets man with what He has made plain—as plain as possible; but it is only as having received the gospel that His word comes fully and properly before us; and if as Christians we desire the wonderful blessing that is for us there, we must with diligence of heart give ourselves to it. "I have esteemed the words of Thy mouth more than my necessary food," says the Psalmist. But our necessary food claims much labor from us. Yet the Lord says, "Labor not for the meat which perisheth but for the meat which endureth unto everlasting life, which the Son of Man shall give unto you."

Given it is: no mere earnestness or toil would avail otherwise, but yet so as to need diligence of heart for its reception. "If thou criest after knowledge, and liftest up thy voice for understanding, if thou seekest her as silver, and searchest for her as for hid treasure, *then* shalt thou understand the fear of the Lord, and find the knowledge of God."

Beloved, if we had but an earthly treasure in our gardens, and did not quite know where it was, would there be a bit of the garden that we would not turn over with pick and spade to get at it? Yet here is heavenly treasure! And with this difference, that there is no uncertainty as to whether our toil will be rewarded. Here truly, "in *all* labor there is profit:" that is, of course, if faith be mixed with it.

Now it is because I believe that God's Word has in it immensely more than any thing we have ever found,—because the Lord has in His goodness shown me a little of this, because He has given me to find a road in a new direction into His blessed Word, and which gives, I am sure, views of it which should and will attract and minister to our souls as we travel it,—it is on this account I desire to bring before you what He has shown me. My real desire is that the Word itself in its fulness may be ours,—that we may possess ourselves more of what are our choicest possessions. May God by His Spirit, who alone can, and for His Son's sake, grant it to us!

Now let me show you briefly how the Lord led me into this, and this will at the same time give us much of the Scripture proof. You will test by it all that is said,—prove all things, hold fast what is good. To the judgment of the Word I desire unfeignedly to submit every thing that may be uttered.

Some years since, now, I was engaged in the study of the Psalms as a whole. I had been made painfully to feel how little I knew of a book which is the very heart of the Old Testament, and in which all the people of God at all times have found language for some of the deepest emotions of their souls. I knew, of course, as all Christians do, certain parts of the book, and had found, as all have, what was of the greatest interest and profit too; yet as to the *whole*, I have often compared the view I had to what one might have of a line of coast lying in a fog, points sticking out here and there, sunny and attractive, and you are sure there is connecting land between, only you do not see it. I longed for this fog to rise, and took up the book to seek out more the connection of psalm with psalm, and thus, as I believed, the place and power of each.

While pursuing this with the best help obtainable, two things became plain, which soon united to lead me into new thoughts, not only as to the Psalms, but as to the whole of Scripture. I began to see that there was a methodical *structure* throughout, and that this had to do with the *meaning* of what was there.

One of the two things I speak of I was led to through a remark I found in a well-known critical commentary—that of Franz Delitzsch,—that the Jews called the book of Psalms the "*Pentateuch of David.*"

You have now in the Revised Version that division into five books, which is found in the Hebrew, and which makes the Psalms a Pentateuch, or whole of five parts. But it is not merely the fact of such a division which is conveyed by such a term. Delitzsch himself admits in a certain way that the arrangement of the books was guided by a purpose of "imitation of the Thora" (the Law); and that "it was *perhaps* this which led to the opening of the fourth book, which corresponds to the book of Numbers, with a psalm of Moses of this character,—the ninetieth psalm. Of psalm cvii.

at the beginning of the fifth book, he also says, " Now, just as in the book of Deuteronomy Israel stands on the threshold of the land of promise, after the two tribes and a half have already established themselves on the other side of Jordan, so at the beginning of this fifth book of the Psalter we see Israel restored to the soil of its fatherland. There, it is the Israel redeemed out of Egypt; here, it is the Israel redeemed out of the land of the exile. There, the lawgiver once more admonishes Israel to yield the obedience of love to the law of Jehovah; here, the Psalmist calls upon Israel to show gratitude toward Him who has redeemed it from exile, and distress, and death."

The resemblance is fuller than Delitzsch makes it; but seeing so much, is it not a wonder to find him stop and look no further into the matter? He is on a track which would open the Psalms to him from end to end: what hinders him from pursuing it? Plainly enough, a lack of faith in a divine superintendence of all this: " A psalm of Moses was placed first, in order to give a *pleasing relief* to the beginning of a new psalter by this glance back to the earliest time" ! Manifestly, if that is all, there is nothing divine in it. So the clue is lost, and never regained by him.

But it led me further; simply because that in making me see the resemblances, he had convinced me that they were *of God*. And I soon found that as the psalm of the wilderness opened the fourth book, so a psalm of the *sanctuary*—the seventy-third—opened the third or Leviticus book; followed by other psalms of similar character. More than this, I soon learned that not only a few opening psalms, but the books in every part corresponded, book with book, in these two pentateuchs.

This is not the place for taking up this further. It opened the Psalms to me as I had never seen them; but another discovery united with this to lead me on, and now beyond the book of Psalms itself.

I was arrested by the structure of the alphabetic psalms. Our version is here in general deficient, and with one exception, the nine psalms of this character have nothing to mark them out as such to the English reader. The hundred and nineteenth psalm is this one exception; and even here, many are not aware that the letters of the Hebrew alphabet, which are found at the head of each section in it, are intended to notify us of the fact that each of these letters begins the eight verses of the section which it heads. There are twenty-two letters in the alphabet, and twenty-two sections in the psalm. Thus the psalm runs through the alphabet: twenty-two sections of always eight verses each.

Why, then, this strange peculiarity? If the Psalms were only a human composition, we should not care much to consider. Poets write acrostics, and it is a mere question of good or bad taste,—sometimes indeed an aid to the memory; but if this be of God, and the Spirit of God has written an acrostic, can we afford to pass it lightly by? Is there not,—must there not be,—meaning in the very form?

Can we gather a meaning? This number 8 written upon the whole psalm has a significance of its own in Scripture. Where used in types, it speaks of the beginning of a new period, the first day of a new week, and in general of what is *new* in contrast with the old which has passed away. It may thus mark the new creation, the *new covenant*, etc.

Now it flashed upon me—What is this hundred and nineteenth psalm? It is the longest psalm in the Bible, beautifully noteworthy as such, for it is throughout the *praise of the law*. It follows the hundred and eighteenth psalm, in which the Jews are viewed prophetically as receiving Christ. They say, as the Lord declares they will say, "Blessed is He that cometh in the name of the Lord," and the "stone which the builders rejected" becomes the "head of the corner." Hence, yielding their hearts to God, they break out in praise of the law. Every letter of man's speech is used to celebrate it, and this number 8, stamped on the whole, is the *new-covenant number*, for "I will write My laws upon their hearts" is a *promise of the new covenant*.

Here, then, is a new thought gained: the structure of the psalm has impressed upon it *a number in harmony with its spiritual meaning*. If this be a law of Scripture, how important to have reached this law!

Does this psalm stand alone? Though our Bibles give no hint of it, every commentary, however brief, will assure the least critical that there are nine of these alphabetic psalms—often more or less irregular, but still evidently that; and with *method even in their irregularity*.

Take, to begin with, two psalms that stand together —the one hundred and eleventh and one hundred and twelfth psalms. In your Bibles you will find they have, not twenty-two, but only ten verses each. If you look more closely, you will see that in both psalms, eight verses are—as in general the verses are in the poetical books—composed of two parts each. This gives sixteen parts: we need six more to make up the twenty-two, and the last two verses are composed of *three* parts each, just completing the proper number. The letters of the alphabet stand in regular order at the beginning of these twenty-two parts.

That these psalms correspond thus exactly with one another is our assurance that there is *method* in it; but here there is no irregularity. If we look at the twenty-fifth and thirty-fourth psalms, we shall find what would be called irregularity, but even in this, the one is precisely similar to the other. In each, one letter, and the same one—the letter "V," is dropped, and the alphabet, so far defective, ends with the twenty-first verse. But there is a concluding verse—a twenty-second, and in each psalm again this begins, not with the omitted letter, but with the letter "P."

Now I cannot explain this, but who that would treat God's Word with reverence would not say, There must be design in it? If design, then, whose is the design? —but let us still proceed.

In the ninth and tenth psalms, we find again an alphabetic structure, but this time with much more irregularity. Here, *one* alphabet runs through the *two* psalms, and unites them together. There are certain omissions which I need not dwell upon in the ninth psalm. The tenth begins regularly with the needed "L," but there it stops: from the second to the eleventh verse inclusive there is no trace of alphabet. Six letters are gone, although the six divisions representing them are there. Then with the twelfth verse, "Arise, O Lord," the alphabet begins again, and from this it goes on regularly to the end of the psalm.

This tenth psalm has naturally been a cause of trouble to the commentators. They did not know what had become of the missing letters. There was an apparent confusion in it which did not seem as if it could be designed at all. Some have set it down to mere inability in the writer to carry out his plan all through. Some, with more reverence, have imagined an accident to the psalm in its transmission, and Bishop Horsley tried to rearrange the verses so as to get the alphabet in order, as he thought it must have been at first; but it would not yield itself to his management at all. Because the psalm as it stands is perfect, and the apparent disorder is designed.

Can we interpret it? In measure, at least, beloved friends, I think we can. The two psalms are connected in matter as in structure, and the common subject is, The day of the Lord,—God's triumph over the wicked in the last days. The tenth psalm takes up especially one wicked one, who comes into terrible prominence in the prophecies of those days. I need not speak more of him, for my purpose is not at all interpretation now, but I want you to notice that it is just the description of this wicked one which occupies the gap in this alphabetic structure of the psalm. Before it comes to him, there is regularity of structure. After the description of him is ended, there is regularity again. But when he is before the view, the order of the psalm is apparently destroyed. Beneath the surface it is still there: the six divisions answering to the letters are all there, although the letters them-selves are absent; there is an apparent interruption of God's ways,—only apparent. Patiently He seems to endure the evil,—"keeping silence," as He Himself expresses it,—until the due time of judgment comes, the harvest-time for which all has been ripening. Then His purposes, never set aside, come into open light. How significantly the structure speaks here, and what order is in this disorder!

But it is not only in the Psalms that we find such things as these. The book of Lamentations is another very striking example. Of course I refer to the Hebrew, for the English version is as silent here as elsewhere. The book of Lamentations is written in a very singular way. There are five chapters, and these are very distinctly marked as divisions in the Hebrew. You may notice that each chapter, except the third, has twenty-two verses—just the number of the letters of the alphabet again. The *third* chapter has sixty-six verses—22 multiplied by 3, *the number of the chapter itself*. In the first and second chapters, we have once more a regular alphabetic structure. One letter stands at the beginning of each verse in regular order. In the third chapter, as I have said already, there are sixty-six verses, each letter being repeated three times. In the fourth, we have another single alphabet; in the fifth, again, the same number of verses, but no alphabet at all.

I simply call attention to this now, and the structure of the third chapter is specially important. It seems to show that a third section is pressed upon our attention *as* a third. It is intimated to us that this is significant;

and if we could look into the chapter, we should find once more that in fact the number impressed upon the structure is in harmony with its spiritual meaning. But this we are not prepared to do just now.

Is this the way then, in which Scripture is written? or are these merely exceptional instances? Beloved friends, when a man, prospecting for ore, comes upon a seam of metal on the surface of a rock, he does not readily believe that that which comes just before his eyes is all that is to be found there. And geologists have remarked upon the special providential care that has tilted up and broken across the strata of the earth, as it were, just to make known to man the stores more deeply packed away. Had they lain just as, ages ago, they were deposited, we might forever have been igno. rant of the wealth lying in the bowels of the earth for us. And has not God in these scriptures just exposed to us, as it were, the heads of precious veins which lie deeper? Would He not have us follow them out, and see to what they lead? Is it not worth while? Surely it is not a meaningless thing if the Spirit of God has been pleased to adopt man's fashion and write acrostics. The strangeness of it should invite our attention. Alas! instead of following them out, we have refused to recognize in this strange human guise the God who comes to meet us thus, and once more dropped out of our hands a clue that would have led us on to wealth of blessing.

Can we find, then, a similar structure elsewhere where no alphabetic mark is given to indicate it? That is very soon answered. Let any one take up, for instance, the second psalm. You will note that it has

twelve verses. And these verses, let us remember, are
not, as in the prose parts of Scripture, arbitrary divisions too often, a convenience merely for making the
text accessible for ready reference; but real verses,
necessitated by the text itself, and accepted by every
scholar and critic the world over. There are twelve
verses, then. The subject of the psalm is God's ap-
pointment of Christ to be king in Zion, in spite of the
opposition of the nations to it. The first verses are
quoted by the apostles in the Acts, "Lord, Thou art
God, which hast made heaven and earth, and the sea,
and all that in them is; who by the mouth of Thy
servant David hast said, 'Why did the heathen rage,
and the people imagine vain things? The kings of the
earth stood up, and the rulers took counsel together
against the Lord, and against His Christ.'" And
thus they apply this: "For of a truth, against Thy
holy child Jesus, whom Thou hast anointed, both
Herod and Pontius Pilate, with the Gentiles, and the
people of Israel, were gathered together, to do what-
soever Thy hand and Thy counsel determined before
to be done."

Now if you will look at the twelve verses of this
psalm, you will see very easily that there is a regular
division indicated by the subject. It is divided into
sections of three verses each: the first giving the re-
bellious attitude of the nations; the second, Jehovah's
attitude; the third, Christ Himself declaring the de-
cree; the fourth, the exhortation to the kings of earth
to submit to Him during the time of his long-suffering.

A regular structure is apparent here; but not only
so, the verses of the psalm are twelve in number; but

twelve has been taken by many before myself to be the governmental number: the psalm, we cannot doubt, is a psalm of divine government. Hence we find another exemplification of the law I have mentioned, that the *number impressed upon the structure of a scripture* corresponds with and points out its *spiritual meaning*.

We might go through many a passage by way of illustration and proof that the alphabetic psalms only bring to the surface, as it were, a character of Scripture found where there is no alphabet whatever. The fifth psalm gives another example of the same structure as the second. The seventy-sixth is again another. The one hundred and thirty-ninth psalm has twenty-four verses, and these divide into four parts of six verses each. The fifty-third of Isaiah, to which the last three verses of the fifty-second admittedly belong, gives thus fifteen verses, which fall regularly into five sections of three verses each. But it would not be profitable here to pursue this. *Regularity* of structure, let it be noted also, is **found** comparatively seldom. A given number of verses may be divided in various ways, and each mode of division be perfectly fitted for the expression of the truth contained. What is maintained is simply that in every part of Scripture a significant structure exists, the significance of which is in some expressed number, to be interpreted by the ordinary meaning of that number, as elsewhere found in Scripture.

And this applies, not only to the smaller divisions, but to the grand divisions of the Bible no less,—to books, and divisions of books, wherever divisions can be shown. The numerical seal is impressed upon every part,—a witness of the perfection of every part, as well as a guide in its interpretation. It is plain that if this be true, it has exceeding importance. The proof of it is only begun at present; and before it can be rightly given, it is evident that we must first of all look at, closely and with care, the meanings of the numbers themselves. Unless there is some precision as to these, the locks we seek to open will not yield themselves to the key.

Before, however, we devote ourselves to this inquiry, allow me a few brief words upon what is indeed not Scripture, but what we cannot therefore dismiss in that way as of no importance to it. By the Word of God all things were made; yea, "without Him was not any thing made that was made." The Word of God is He by whom God is told out. Thus God is made known in all His handiwork. True, the knowledge of Him thus is not sufficient where sin has come in, as it has into this world of ours. And, moreover, dim are our eyes to see what exists, except as they are controlled and guided by revelation. Yet what Christian doubts that there is real agreement between God's work and word, or the confirmation of both as His that is found in this agreement? The physical world,—scarred as it is by the entrance of sin,—yet gives us plentiful proof that it is an orderly scene, still obedient and witnessing to the hand that made it. Winds and waves are not in rebellion against Him. "Its laws," as a noted skeptic has it, "must be His laws." There is system, method, throughout: one God, not working capriciously, but according to His wisdom, and so as to display Himself to His creatures.

Now of old, the wise could affirm that God "looketh

to the ends of the earth, and seeth under the whole heaven, to make *the weight for* the winds, and to weigh the waters by measure" (Job xxviii. 25). And the prophet, centuries after, challenges on God's part, "Who hath measured the waters in the hollow of his hand, and meted out heaven with a span, and comprehended the dust of the earth in a measure, and weighed the mountains in scales, and the hills in a balance?" (Is. xl. 12.) But who could have anticipated how modern science would find in these weights and measurements the key to a very large part of all its knowledge? Weights and measures! what would chemistry, for instance, do without these? Sir John Herschel says, "Chemistry is, in a most pre-eminent degree, the science of quantity, and to enumerate the discoveries which have arisen for it from the *mere determination of weights and measures* would be nearly to give a synopsis of this branch of knowledge." But he goes further than this, and affirms, "Indeed, it is a character of *all the higher laws of nature* to assume the form of a precise *quantitive* statement."

This means that the numerical structure which we have begun to trace in Scripture pervades all nature no less than Scripture. How profoundly interesting to find it so! And in this case, no man of science will ever question it. Another celebrated man, Alexander von Humboldt, declares that "it may be said that the only remaining and widely diffused hieroglyphic characters still in our writing—*numbers*—appear to us again as *powers of the cosmos*, although in a wider sense than that applied to them by the Italian school."

But if so, how striking to find that they are powers

in Scripture as well as in the world! and yet what more natural?

Let us look at a few facts, well known, but which may serve to impress us more with the reality of all this. Chemistry, it has been already said, is pre-emi-nently the science of quantity—*i. e.*, of numbers. Every element known has its distinct combining number. For instance, if we speak of oxygen, its number is 16. This means that in every compound in which oxygen is found, it is either just sixteen parts by weight of this, or some multiple of this, as 32, 64, etc. And so with all the elements.

Not only so, but certain of these elements may be easily made to form a series differing from each other by some fixed number, or multiplies of it, and this seems to mark some family likeness between the numbers of such a series. Thus, fluorine, chlorine, bromine, iodine, have real likeness, and their combining numbers are, 17, 35, 80, 125. These numbers differ from each other by multiples of 9.

Chemistry, then, dealing with the very foundations of the world, finds there this numerical stamp upon every stone in it. And how much more may be any day added to our knowledge! So much is known as makes it easy to predict that every advance will be in this direction.

Botany and zoology cannot be said as yet to show just the same susceptibility to numerical law. Yet even here there have been those who believed in a definite numerical proportion of groups and species. I shall have to quote from one of these writers somewhat at another time; but it seems, at least, most probable that explorations in this line would be attended with the best success. A narrow conception seems most to have baffled previous attempts. Most certainly, if it were attempted to prove that all *Scripture* divided into a fixed number of sections, a number which ruled in every division and every subdivision of these to the very smallest, nothing could result but disappointment. Yet a numerical system obtains, none the less, throughout the Word; but freer, broader, and greater in conception than this, whose narrowness would destroy at once all spiritual significance.

Be this as it may, as to these sciences, there is yet plenty to show that numbers are in them still at any rate "powers of the cosmos." In both, we find certain numbers attaching themselves to certain groups, and series of numbers in definite proportion to one another. Thus we find the number 2 prevailing among mosses; 3 and its multiples, among endogens, such as the lilies; 5, among the exogenous of netted veined plants. In the arrangement of leaves upon the stem, a law of proportion prevails which is of a very striking character. There is clearly nothing haphazard about it. All leaves will be found situated in the course of an upward spiral which winds round the stem. Scales on a disk and flowers on a disk are similarly placed. "These spirals are not the same, and are defined by the number of circuits round the stem as contrasted with the number of leaves in the circuits considered. We have thus the fractions, $\frac{1}{2}$, $\frac{1}{3}$, $\frac{2}{5}$, $\frac{3}{8}$, *each succeeding fraction being formed by the addition of the numerators and denominators of the two preceding ones*, as the formula of these relations. The fraction $\frac{1}{2}$ expresses one circuit and two leaves; the fraction ⅓, one circuit and three leaves. The remaining fractions are combinations of these two. Two-fifths represents two circuits and five leaves; ⅜, three circuits and eight leaves," etc.

These proportions are very singular. To us, they have, indeed no precise significance. It is only in Scripture at present that we find definite speech in numbers. Yet they show none the less that there is a pervading use of them in nature which is certainly designed and of God. If we found but so many stones arranged in rows or circles in just these proportions, we should be assured that mind had been at work in it. Here, we may be surer, if possible, that the Infinite mind has been at work.

As to zoology, all that I have to say of it I shall reserve for a little further on. It is a field little worked as yet in the direction indicated, and it will be only what is to be expected if its numerical system be more complicated and recondite, less easy to be grasped than that of lower forms. Still there are intimations sufficient to assure us that there is no lack of harmony between zoology and her sister sciences.

Helped and strengthened, then, by these witnesses from the works of God around, let us now go back to the Word, to learn the language of these numerals, which are then to be the interpreters of so much else.

LECTURE II

THE SCRIPTURE NUMERALS

REVELATION, beloved brethren, I am happy to think that you will fully agree with me, is the key to every thing in nature. I do not mean, of course, that nature is absolutely dumb without it. If I said so, I should be contradicting revelation. "The invisible things of Him from the creation of the world are clearly seen, being understood by the things that are made, even His eternal power and Godhead." "The heavens declare the glory of God, and the firmament showeth His handiwork. Day unto day showeth speech, and night unto night telleth knowledge." True, surely, all that is. What I mean is, that while parts of the lesson of creation are thus learned, they are but fragments of comparatively external knowledge. To the whole as a whole, and to the deepest, fullest, sweetest, of all its teachings we must remain strangers, except we will take revelation to introduce us to them. And if we would do this, what preachers would all things about us become? How would all things be transfigured for us!

Take one of the chief mysteries of creation. Ask the greatest of heathen sages,—ask the men whose glory it is to have emancipated themselves (vain thought!) from the Christianity they had inherited from their fathers, How is it that every where through creation *death is the food of life?* They will turn the question back to you with a sarcasm or a scoff. With the Mahometan, but without his reverence, they may say, perhaps, "It has so pleased God." But revelation lights up the mystery. Yes, the wail of death is every where, true! It *has* pleased God, wherever we look, to hang out the warning before *his* eyes to whom death is a penalty and a dread. But it is not a lesson of judgment merely: "out of death, life" is the law of sacrifice. The Jewish altars do but repeat more solemnly the symbolism of nature. The Christian finds the veil removed in Christ.

Take another instance: "God," says the apostle, "is light." And the man of science preaches to us that light is a trinity of color, bathing all nature with varied brilliance, according as each object reflects partially what it receives. For it *receives* it: the world's light is from heaven, not self-developed; and practically from the sun. The sun, preaches the scientist, is the great reservoir of force to the globes which roll in their orbits round it, bound by invisible cords, which the faith permitted to men by science recognizes. But what *is* the sun? It is essentially, the same teachers tell us, what the earth is; but this the light clothes with its glory,—separable from it, but not separate. And God manifest in the flesh, says the Christian, that is Christ, the "Sun of Righteousness."

How much of the mystery of things would pass into glory in which we should be worshipers, if only we realized that creation is a perpetual object-lesson of things which the Word of God alone reveals to us. But this is not an authority for men of science; they have given up "bibliolatry,"—the worship of a book. It is ruled out; and therein they have ruled out all their highest wisdom, and have fallen into folly.

When we take up the numerals, to ascertain from Scripture their significance, we shall find, on the other hand, what I have only recently begun in any proper way to realize, that this significance of theirs has its roots in nature. Scripture must control and guide our thoughts, or they will be what poor human thoughts are apart from God. Nevertheless, the spiritual does not abhor what is natural, except it be in the sense of what is fleshly, the product of the fall. The first four numbers, at least, are distinctly dependent for the meaning which Scripture gives them upon their natural significance; and from these, all others are built up. It is no great wonder this: it is simply to say that Scripture uses them as what they are. And this is just the beautiful harmony and propriety of Scripture. Everything is in its place: used of God, and illuminated by its use; not arbitrarily applied, and never perverted.

A word or two upon this, because of its importance, before we go on. How wise and appropriate are the Baptist's words when the priests and Levites from Jerusalem asked him why he baptized. Pharisees they were: men who baptized their hands always before eating, lest their souls should be defiled. Note, then, the wisdom of the reply, " John answered them, saying, ' I baptize with *water*.' " Did they not know that? Of course they did. And did not they themselves baptize with water, when they ceremonially washed their hands? Ah, that is just the question. Does the ritualist baptize with *water*, when he changes a babe's sinful nature by a few drops upon the face? Surely it is not in the power of *water* to do this? Well, but this, he thinks, is one of the mysteries of Christianity, and the water is *sanctified* to the washing away of sin! Well, that is exactly what John's quiet words deny. This is not mystery, but magic. Water is *water*, and God uses it as that, never puts it out of its place; never treats sin as a material thing to be cleansed away after this fashion; never exalts water into a spiritual power; never confounds the spiritual realm with the material. John's baptism was with *water*, and not an intrusion on the spiritual realm of Christ.

But to return to our numerals. It is only of late that I have seen how few the numbers are which need interpreting. Seven notes in music give us the capacity for the almost infinite variety and harmony of song. The eighth note is but the octave—a first repeated in a higher key. Just so there are seven numbers which have significance in Scripture. Seven is the number of perfection, and we cannot go beyond perfection; although, of course, there may be here, too, a lower and a higher scale. The number 8, at which we have already glanced, is that which we have seen to speak of a new beginning, which just shows the series to be finished. It is the spiritual octave.

We have seven numbers, then, really to consider. Of course I am aware that beyond this there are special numbers which have significance, as, for instance, 10, and 12, and 40. These we shall speak of, if the Lord will. But the meaning attached to them is really only the combined meaning of the numbers which are their factors; 10, for instance, of 5 and 2; 12, of 4 and 3:

40, of 4 and 10.   The meaning of these smaller numbers gives us, therefore, in reality, the whole meaning
of the numerals of Scripture.

1.

To begin, then, with the number 1.   What does it stand
for?   When it is said, "Hear, O Israel, the Lord thy
God is one Lord," or when it says, "And the Lord
shall be King over all the earth ; in that day there shall
be one Lord, and His name one," we have the simple,
primary thought of unity, the exclusion of difference.

But this may be in two ways ; in the two quotations
just made, the difference is external : there is no other
Lord, there shall be no other.   It is an assertion of independency, as admitting no other; and implies, of
course, a sufficiency which *needs* no other.   To be in
this way independent, sufficient to Himself, belongs to
God alone.   And thus, under this number 1, we begin
with God.   His title is, "The Beginning ;" and Scripture, in fact, begins with Him.   What can be right
where we do not so begin ?

But then this is not the only application.   We shall
find as we proceed with these numerals that they are, in
the case of every one perhaps, used in a bad sense as
well as in a good.   This is true, not only of the numerals, but of many types beside.   Christ is a lion, and
Satan is a lion ; the birds of heaven are wicked spirits,
and yet the bird that dies in the earthen vessel is again
Christ.   In the case of the numbers we shall have
abundant proof ; and this does not alter in the least
their real significance.   Independence in God is His
necessary perfection ; independence in man is sin and

rebellion. Thus it is a question of application only. The first section of the second psalm, as we have seen, speaks, not of God, but of man, and then of man in independence of God,—the rebellion of the nations.

But there is another way in which the number 1 may speak: it may exclude *internal* difference, may speak of internal harmony of parts or attributes, of self-agreement, perfection in that sense. That is not *one* which is internally divided, it is clear. "The dream is one," says Joseph: there is complete agreement of meaning in it.

And this is, again, in the fullest and highest way, true of God alone. In His perfection there is no preponderance of any attribute, and no defect. His wisdom must be equal to His power; His love equal to His power and wisdom. Thus again this number speaks of Him; and in this way, although it may have a lower application, an evil sense is quite impossible.

Now if we turn from the cardinal number to the ordinal, the "First" is again a divine title. It speaks plainly of priority, whether in time or rank, of supremacy; as the Sovereign Beginning of all things, of the Creator, the Source of life. His is the will from which all proceeded; His is the plan according to which all is guided; His is the power by which all is executed: election, counsel, sovereign sway, are all His own.

Thus the number 1 has three meanings essentially,— of independency, unity, and supremacy. These things are in the truest and highest way only true of God. We may find them, however, either united under it or separate, and in this latter way in lower applications, and even evil ones; although comparatively seldom in the latter. God and good are one. Evil is contradiction, discord; in the end, weakness and defeat. Blessed be God it is so!

Now before we take up other numbers, I desire to bring before you, in the briefest way, of course, as illustrating it, the character of the first book of the Pentateuch—Genesis.

It is plain that if there be any truth in that view of Scripture which I am here presenting, the five books of the Pentateuch *ought* to illustrate these numbers, and confirm our use of them. If they do not you will be entitled—nay, necessitated to set down this use as visionary and human merely. If they do, it will go far toward proving that they are divine. It will be important, therefore, to examine them.

Moreover, I am convinced, and fully hope to convince you, that the Pentateuch—assailed as it is by so many at the present day,—is in fact the very basis of the structure of the whole Bible. It is thus additionally a necessity to bring out the character of it, for with it we shall have to compare a large part of Scripture. At this time also the examination will help to fix upon our minds the significance of the numerals themselves, essential as this is to our whole examination

Now what is the first thing that would strike any of us as to the book of Genesis? I suppose that it is, in it we find the story of *creation*. I need not say how fully this agrees with the number we have been considering.

How much this includes within it will be plain if we

consider it: supremacy, election, counsel, are all implied, and Genesis in all its parts brings out these.

1. *Supremacy.* "The Almighty" is the name by
which God revealed Himself to the patriarchs, as He
declared to Moses (Ex. vi. 3). It is found six times
in the book of Genesis, only three times in the Pentateuch beside. In the book of Job it is used largely,
but only eight times in the Old Testament beside. It
is clearly characteristic of the book, therefore.

2. *Election.* Genesis is surely the very book of election. I do not mean that the *doctrine* is found: we
shall not find it in any of these early books; but the
fact is every where. Abraham (and Israel his seed),
Isaac, Jacob, whose lives fill a large part of the book,
are all examples of it. They are the very ones that
the apostle brings forward in the ninth of Romans.

3. *Counsel.* Genesis has been often called the seed-
plot of the Bible. Every thing almost in the revealed
counsels of God finds its place in it in some way; and
at the outset, in the six days' work, we find prefigured,
not only the work of God in individual souls, but the
dispensational steps of blessing, closing with that
which is beyond all dispensations—that rest of God
into which we labor to enter.

Again, the time of the Genesis-history is emphatic-
ally that of the age of promise. The promise of the
woman's Seed is what shines with starlike radiance
over the first part, followed in the second by the
covenant with Abraham, which, the apostle assures us,
the law, coming four hundred and thirty years afterward, could never hamper with conditions. Sovereignty
in blessing thus marks the period throughout.

It is evident that these are features of the book, as it is also that they answer to the numerical place of the book. The key fits the lock thoroughly. It is not that certain things in it can be taken and made to apply: that, no doubt, would be easy enough to do any where; but the point is, that the numerical structure brings out *just what are its characteristic features.* And so it is always, and this is what shows its design, and proves it to be of God. It could not *be*, unless it were designed to be.

2.

We now come to the number 2, and here we have plainly the contrast and opposite of the first number. If 1 excludes difference, 2 affirms it. If 1 says there is not another, 2 says, of course, there is another. And this note of *difference* runs through all its meanings. "Difference" means, in some sort, contrast, easily passing into opposition, contradiction. Two is the first number that *divides :* hence it stands for enmity, conflict. When first studying the Psalms in this way it was that I first noticed how, commonly when I came to a second series, or the second psalm in a series, I found the subject to be the *enemy*. This was before I saw that it was a meaning of the number itself. Of course this is only one side of the number, the bad one.

The other side is essentially the thought of *help*, confirmation, fellowship. The fundamental text here is Eccles. iv.—"Two are better than one; because they have a good reward for their labor. For if they fall, the one will lift up his fellow : but woe to him that is alone when he falleth ; for he hath not another to help him up. Moreover, if two lie together, then they have heat; but how shall one be warm alone? And if one prevail against him, two shall withstand him." That is a thought which again is clearly native in the number; for we speak of " seconding " in the sense of " assisting." I may add that there is involved in it the thought of taking an inferior place in doing so.

How beautifully all this unites in Him who is the second Person of the Godhead, who has taken, in order to befriend our souls, the place of deepest humiliation! In Him, God has laid help upon One that is mighty, and the Son of God has become Christ, the Saviour. Saviour, salvation, in some sense, is thus connected commonly with this number 2. We shall find abundant proof as we go on.

Another meaning connected with it, intimately united with the thought of help, confirmation, is that of competent testimony. "The testimony of two men is true." I would like you to notice also how still the thought of difference enters into this meaning. For *what* makes the competency of two witnesses more than one? It is just this, that the witnesses are different. In rroportion as they are so—different in character, interests, prejudices and prepossessions perhaps, so is their testimony, if nevertheless agreeing, satisfactory and convincing. You may notice it even in God's testimony in His Word. Our Bibles have two parts,—the Old Testament, or Covenant, and the New: these are God's twofold, competent testimony to men; but how different! how contrasted, in many ways! Judaism, ritualistic, restricted, the vail over God's glory in Moses' face; Christianity, with its free grace going out to all, the vail rent, and the glory of God in the unvailed face of Jesus! Yet this is what makes the testimony so complete. How they fit one another ¡ How that old revelation in the hands of the Jew condemns him in rejecting this glorious lifting of the vail in Christianity!

And notice, the second Person of the Godhead is, again, the true Witness, and the Word of God.

If now we take the second book of the Pentateuch, the great features of it are conspicuous enough, and conspicuously illustrate the numerical law of Scripture. Exodus is the book of salvation, which of course infers the enemy from whose power they are delivered. After the blood has redeemed Israel, God comes down in the pillar of cloud and fire to be with them, and the wondrous tale of deliverance gathers fresh features continually. Then comes Sinai and the breach of the golden calf, and the intercession of the mediator, Moses, type of the great Mediator. The tabernacle of testimony and the priesthood complete the picture of God with them.

Before we go on to the next number, I have again an illustration from natural things which has greatly interested me, and which I hope may have equal interest for you. Comparatively recently, I picked up at a bookstore, second hand, a book on the Geography and Classification of Animals, published in 1835. My interest in it was that I knew it contained what professed to be a Natural System of Classification, first brought forward by Mr. McLeay some sixteen years previously, but revised by his disciple, William Swainson, in the volume I speak of.

Now a truly natural system would give us the analogies and affinities of animals as they really exist, and thus the divine plan of creation to some extent; this was my interest in it. I knew it to be also a numerical system, and in this way also was interested in it.

Of the system itself I need say little. That there is truth in it, I believe, though with many defects, on the ground of one of which Agassiz, in his well-known Essay on Classification, sets it aside as unworthy of serious examination,—a judgment, I believe, too severe and sweeping, he himself commending the ability displayed in it (in matters essentially connected with its main subject) in other parts of the same essay.

Swainson's view is, that there are throughout the animal kingdom, in every natural group, three divisions actually and five apparently. The three actual divisions are, the typical, the subtypical, and the aberrant. These stand, with him, as 1, 2, and 3; and while he sees nothing in the numbers *as such*, yet these are the characters he gives to his first two groups :—

" The first distinction of typical groups is implied by the name they bear. The animals they contain are the most perfectly organized; that is to say, they are endowed with the greatest number of perfections, and capable of performing to the greatest extent the functions which peculiarly characterize their respective circles. This is universal in all typical groups; but there is a marked difference between the types of a typical circle and the types of an aberrant one. In the first, we find a combination of properties concentrated, as it were, in certain individuals, without any one of these preponderating in a remarkable degree over the others; whereas in the second it is quite the reverse: in these last, one faculty is developed in the highest degree, as if to compensate for the total absence or very slight development of others " (*p.* 242).

Let any one recall what has been said as to the number 1, and he will see how really this idea of a typical or *first* group agrees with what was stated then. This combination of balanced attributes is just what gives the thought of internal *oneness :* nothing in excess, nothing deficient. Yet Swainson says not a word, evidently has not a thought of this. But in his account of the subtypical or *second* groups, the numerical stamp as I have given it is still more striking, if not more apparent :—

"II. Subtypical groups, as the name implies, are a degree lower in organization than those last described ; and thus exhibit an intermediate character between typical and aberrant divisions. They do not comprise the largest individuals in bulk, but always those which are the most *powerfully armed*, either for inflicting injury on their own class, for exciting terror, producing injury, or creating annoyance to man. Their dispositions are often sanguinary ; since the forms most conspicuous among them live by rapine, and subsist on the blood of other animals. They are, in short, symbolically the types of *evil ;* and in such an extraordinary way is this principle modified in the smaller groups, that even among insects where no other power is possessed but that of causing annoyance or temporary pain, we find in the subtypical order of the *Annulosa*, the different races of scorpions, acari, spiders, and all those repulsive insects whose very aspect is forbidding, and whose bite or sting is often capable of inflicting serious bodily injury" (*pp.* 245, 246).

Now it certainly seems to me that this coincidence of view proceeds from its being truth. My own was derived from Scripture simply, Mr. Swainson's from nature only. He follows a numerical order without perceiving or imagining any thing in the numerals themselves. That there should be in these two cases so real an agreement is surprising, considering the different way by which they have been reached. And this may help to fill the gap left in the proof of a numerical system as regards zoology.

We now come to the number—

3.

And what does 3 intimate to us naturally? Suppose I were to write upon the board here any number you please, it may be 3 itself, and now I put on the right hand upper corner of this a little ^{3} (3^3)—what would every school-boy say I meant by it? He would say I meant 3 *cubed:* that little ^{3} stands for the *cube*—for cubic measure.

And what is cubic measure? It is *solid* measure, the measure of contents. Take any two dimensions, and multiply them together; what have you? A measure of surface merely. Take a third dimension; now you have more than surface : this third dimension strikes in deep below the surface, and gives you a measure of *solidity*.

Three stands then for what is solid, real, substantial, —for fullness, actuality. What are length and breadth without thickness? There is not such a thing in the world : a line that you draw upon paper is more than that. Therefore I say that 3 stands for actuality, reality, realization.

Three is the number of the divine fullness. And in Christ dwelleth all the fullness of the Godhead bodily; what, then, is the measure of the Man Christ Jesus? A beautiful figure of this you will find twice in Scripture. Abraham puts meal before his heavenly guests; and the woman of the parable puts her leaven into meal. Now what is the food which you can put before God Himself and expect Him to be at the table with you? It is Christ upon whom if we feed, communion with God is secured. Christ is the bread of life; and Christ is, as the Revised Version calls it very well now, the *Meal*-Offering. And what is it that is in the woman's (the Church's) hands, but just again this *meal*-offering.

But there was to be no *leaven* put into the meal-offering: she is putting leaven! What is just that which claims most decisively to be Church-teaching? Alas! it is *leavened meal*.

But what is the measure of Christ? Only a Man? No: you have no Christ if you have but that measure of meal. "*Three* measures of meal" in the woman's hand: "three measures of meal" in Abraham's feast; beside that young calf, tender and good, which had yielded up its life. "All the fullness of God" in the Man Christ Jesus; and His death our life!

Three is the number of the Trinity; and the *third* Person in the Godhead is the Holy Spirit. Note, then, that whether in creation or in new creation, He it is who *realizes* all the counsels of God. "By His Spirit He garnished the heavens." When the deep lay over

THE SCRIPTURE NUMERALS   39

the waste and desolate earth, the " Spirit of God
brooded over the waters." When men are born again
to God, the gospel comes to them, " not in word only,
but in power, and in the Holy Ghost." What is sanctification, as the work of the Spirit, but that in which
salvation is *actualized* in the soul? Thus this number 3
has its significance all through, and without the work
of the Spirit there is nothing but outside work : " that
which is born of the Spirit is spirit;" that is the third
dimension which every saint has.

And the sanctuary, God's dwelling-place,—that too
is a *cube;* ten cubits in the tabernacle; twenty in the
temple. The final city, which the glory of God
lightens, is a cube also : " the length and the breadth
and the height of it are equal." How strange for the
dimensions of a city ! How blessed to think of *there*
the counsels of God now realized, the holiness He
seeks attained !

In the sanctuary God manifests Himself; with the
third Person of the Godhead, the Unity becomes a
Trinity : Father, Son, and Spirit tell out for the first
time fully God. And 3 is thus the number of *manifestation.* So resurrection is plainly that work of His
where all human power is at an end; and thus
resurrection is on the *third* day.

Now if we turn to Leviticus, the third book of the
Pentateuch, we find full illustration and confirmation
of all this. The tabernacle is just set up, and God
speaks out of the " tent of meeting " where He meets
and welcomes men. The theme of the book is sanctification, and thirty-nine times in connection with the
precepts, of which the latter part of it largely consists,

is appended the word, " I am Jehovah."   Seven times is it repeated, " Be ye holy, for I, the Lord your God, am holy."

At the opening of the book the offerings are opened out, the beauteous picture of Him through whom all sanctification is attained, who is the pattern of it.   In the middle of the book the holiest is opened, to sprinkle the precious blood upon the mercy-seat. Not yet— for these are but the figures of the true,—is the way made for all to draw near to God, but we have in type the foundation of it.

Thus Leviticus shows the numerical stamp as plainly as Genesis and Exodus.   Our convictions that it is of God deepen as we proceed.   And now we have God's name fairly written out upon this book of His.   When we would show a book to be our own, we write our name upon the opening page.   God has written His in three successive pages in the beginning of His Word.   In Genesis, we may say, we have the Father, the Life-giver; in Exodus, the Son, the Saviour; in Leviticus, the Spirit, the Sanctifier.   God's book is fairly claimed as His, and he who would erase the Name must answer it.

LECTURE III

The Numerals Continued

WE have looked at the first three numbers, then, beloved brethren; and these have a peculiar place and eminency in Scripture over the others. No wonder, if they signify what they do. Of course, as the commencement of the series, they must occur more frequently than the others. But that is not all, nor what I mean. There is this distinctive difference between these first three numbers and those which follow them: they are *prime* numbers: not simply in an arithmetical, but in a Scripture sense.

Of course, arithmetically they are prime numbers: they can be divided by no others; but this is as true of 5 and 7 which come afterward, and which are not prime numbers in the Scripture-sense.

For Scripture has its own method of division of these numbers, and we must pay the closest attention to all its methods, if we would obtain the insight into it that we seek. Thus 4, we shall find, divides here not only in the ordinary way, but as 3 and 1 also. Seven divides very commonly indeed into 4 and 3. Five, I believe, also, though the proof is more obscure, into 4 and 1. And the mere fact of the division is not the whole: the numbers obtain their significance from the combined meanings of those into which they divide. Thus the difference between the first three and the rest is as the difference between a primitive and a manufactured article. Very significant indeed it is, in view of what we have been considering, that those now before us have their meaning derived from the former ones, connected as they are with the display of God; for "of Him, and through Him, and to Him, are all things: to whom be glory forever. Amen."

We shall find also that the meanings of these latter are less comprehensive by far. They are more *definite*, for to define is to *limit*. Thus a fourth section is perhaps the easiest of all to recognize. It appeals to us in a sadly intelligible way. Yet, as the minor notes in music, all this falls into the general harmony, and adds an expression to it very sweet and necessary. The shadows outline the landscape, and give it tone and tenderness. Such is God's triumph over sin.

4.

The number 4 is the first one capable of true division, and which the number 2 divides. This gives it its character. It is significant of that which *yields itself up to this division, as material to the hand that fashions it*. It is thus the number of the world, and implies *weakness* necessarily, therefore, which may give way under trial, and yield to another hand than the One who has title over it. And this the creature has done. Therefore the world is what it is to-day, and all the trial and evil of which it is the scene.

Thus we have "four corners of the *earth*," and, as disturbing influences, the "four winds of heaven." The way in which these are used may be well seen in that passage in the seventh of Daniel, in which he says, "Behold, the four great winds of heaven strove upon the great sea, and four great beasts came up from the sea, diverse one from the other." It was indeed amid the encounter of the powers of the earth that the Gentile empires predicted here arose. And such still is the condition of the world through which we pass—a scene of various and constant strife, which is Satan's sieve to sift us with, though God be over all. In this, failure and evil come out plentifully in us, and with this the number commonly, but not necessarily, connects itself.

As I have said, there are two ways in which it is divided in Scripture. Often, as in the four Gospels, it is divided into 3 and 1. The first three gospels are confessedly kindred in view, and widely different from John, which, in the character of truth, and even of its narrative, is a second division rather than a fourth. This we shall hope to examine at another time. A similar division we shall find in other cases. But here, the division of four, the world-number, brings out two of the specially divine ones: 3, the number of divine manifestation; 1, that of the Creator. And this is the ideal result of all the trial of the creature—the manifestation of the Creator. This is what, after all, we find in the world; it is its illuminated side, so to speak. And in a higher way altogether was it true of Him who as Man perfectly glorified God under every possible trial. This is the meaning of the four gospels, and of that division of the four which we have just glanced at.

On the other hand, the seven parables of the kingdom in the thirteenth of Matthew divide, as usually, into 4 and 3. The first four are given in the hearing of the multitude at large; the last three, to disciples in the house. The first four, in accordance with the significance of the number, give the world-aspect, in which the testing and failure of man are seen abundantly; the last three, in similar accordance, give the divine accomplishments, recognized by faith alone.

But these first four parables, as we might expect, are not divided as the gospels are. Here, that other division of the number which I have spoken of is found: the first two parables are clearly to be distinguished from the latter two; in the first, we have individuals simply; in the second, the collective whole. The division is the *true* division arithmetically, from which the significance of the number is derived, and which testifies to the weakness of the creature and the agency of evil.

The proof in all this will appear stronger the more it is considered. As we go on, we shall find it constantly receiving confirmation in ever-increasing proportion to the examples produced. Here, I must limit myself to one other illustration of the number before us, and that will be, as before, by the corresponding book of the Pentateuch, which is the book of Numbers.

Numbers is a book very clear in its general meaning, and its witness for the numerical structure is so much the more evident. It is the history of the wilderness, as one of its Hebrew titles indicates, of Israel's journeyings from Sinai to the land of Moab, over against the promised land, where Deuteronomy gives them its final word. It is essentially *their* history; for though Exodus gives the account of the first part of the way as far as Sinai from the Red Sea, yet its object is very different, namely, to show God's care over them and provision for them, according to the grace of that deliverance which is the theme of the book. And surely Numbers is not wanting in this grace; but that it may *be* grace, the people are permitted to show out fully what they are,—what *we* are, no less than they. Then the resurrection-priesthood displays its virtues for them; and the root of sin being reached and judged in the brazen serpent, the accusation of the enemy is turned into full unchallengeable blessing.

This is in general the character of the book, which typically tells of our pilgrimage to our heavenly land, of the trials and the failure by the way, still of the Shepherd's love and power for us no less, and of the priestly intercession of the One risen out of death, upon which all depends.

5.

In the cleansing of the leper, and in the consecration of the priest alike, the blood is put upon three parts of man, which together manifest what he is,—the tip of the right ear, the thumb of the right hand, and the great toe of the right foot. By the ear he is to receive the word of God; with the hand, to do the enjoined work; with the foot, to walk in His blessed ways. This is evidently the man in his whole responsibility.

Each of these parts is stamped with the number 5.

The ear is the avenue to the higher part; and there are five of such senses, by which man is put in connection with the whole scene around: the avenues of perception, by which alone he can be appealed to.

The hand of man is that by which he moulds and fashions the natural world around him. It is the expression of active power; the four fingers, with an

opposing thumb, the consecrated because the govern-
ing part. These on the two hands give 10, the number of the commandments in the two tables of the law,
the measure of natural responsibility.

The foot, the expression of personal conduct, gives
a similar division, much less marked however, and the
two feet a similar 10. Five stands thus as the number
of man, exercised and responsible, under the government of God.

The 4 and 1, so strikingly marked upon his hands,
the instrument by which he takes hold upon the world
around him, are striking figures, easy to be read in this
connection. They speak of the created world sub-
mitted to its Creator,—of God's government, in short,
itself. Of this, man is in measure, as seen in his hand,
the representative; while *as* the representative, he is
pre-eminently the subject of it.

The exercise of which man is the subject is not alone
as to the path before him, but often also as to the governmental ways of God with him; and although the
Christian now knows God as his Father, yet the exercise remains and is needful. In God's government
still it is true that clouds and darkness are round about
Him, and that we cannot meet Him face to face. Just
on this very account most of all is it that "no chasten-
ing for the present seemeth to be joyous, but grievous;
but *afterward* it yieldeth the peaceable fruit of righteousness unto those who are exercised thereby." How
profitable the earnest searching of heart and inquiry
which may result from God's hidden ways with us, we
are often witness to ourselves.

Under the number 5 we shall find these exercises,

then, and their fruit,—how "tribulation worketh patience, and patience experience, and experience hope." Above all in those didactic books of the Old Testament, which are specially its human voice, in which we find just five books, often, as in the Psalms, dividing into just five books again, beautifully closing in this case with five halleluiahs. For thus our harps of praise are strung and tuned in sorrow.

But we must now learn a little to discriminate. Twelve has been mentioned before as a number speaking of divine government; here we find 5 to speak of it again; and yet again 1 would seem to be the rightful expression of divine supremacy. Is there no collision here? or does it not seem as if these numbers were thus capable of so much latitude as to take away the definiteness we might reasonably look for, and leave them to be moulded by the imagination at its will?

In fact, it is the very reverse, which a comparison of these numbers shows. They reveal, the more we examine them, a delicacy of application which will satisfy the observant mind of the reality of their indications. No doubt their meanings often approach one another, and this is only what we might expect; yet there is never wanting a real distinction which redeems them from all vagueness, and the examination of these three numbers will fully establish this.

One, then, is indeed the number which speaks of supremacy as none else can. This is so obvious that there is no need to dilate upon it much. It is the number, therefore, which speaks of the government or kingdom of God *from its divine side*.

Five, as we have seen, contains this number, but as 4 and 1. This is seen in another way also than in that I have already indicated, and in a way more simply scriptural. For the usual division of 7 in Scripture is 4 *plus* 3; and here we have 4 as a first completed series, and the last three another, which therefore 5 begins. It would in this case be, of course, a 4 *plus* 1. No doubt the proof is here more obscure than usual. A further research may make it clearer, and I believe will.

For what is the meaning of this 4 *plus* 3? It is the world-number, and the number of divine manifestation added to it; and it is when God is thus manifested in connection with His works that He can *rest;* therefore the seventh day is the day of God's rest, and His creation-rest is but the type of the full rest to come.

But if, then, the last three in this 7 be the number of the Trinity—of God fully revealed—it would seem as if it would result that 5 would be a 4 *plus* 1; and 6, a 4 *plus* 2; and that here the former divine numbers would afresh reveal their significance. What can we have, in fact, more than God and the world? What can we expect, then, but a repetition here of the divine 1 and 2? And when this suits and illustrates as it does the meaning otherwise obtained, why should we hesitate to accept it as the true key?

But thus it is no wonder if a shadow of the first number be apparent in the number before us. Five has the meaning of 1 in it, just because indeed it is a 4 *plus* 1. Yet this does not make it a mere repetition. There is this number 4 which stands before it, the number of the world—the creature; and it is from the human side we have approached it therefore. It is, in fact, the *human side of divine government* that is conveyed by it, as the divine side is by the number 1. Thus it speaks, not so much of the *throne* as of the *ways* of God—ways which expressed in commandments, become the guidance and define the responsibility of the creature; while, as they are more strictly ways of a sovereign God, they give him needed exercise, humbling, and so blessing.

As to 12, it lies outside of the series we are considering, but finds its meaning in the numbers which are its arithmetical factors; and these are 4 and 3, not added, of course, but multiplied together. It is only in the relation of the two numbers, therefore, that it differs from 7: the number of the world and of divine manifestation prevail in it; but these are not side by side merely, but acting upon each other. It is God manifesting Himself in the world of His creation as 7 is, but in *active energy laying hold upon* and transforming it. Thus 12 is the number of *manifest* sovereignty, as it was exercised in Israel by the Lord in the midst of them, or as it will be exercised in the world to come, while 1 and 5 apply to His government all through the dispensations—to a throne which is never given up; for he who is not sovereign is not God.

Thus the three numbers have each their distinct sphere and meaning, and the examination cannot but deepen our sense of their precision and power of utterance. We have yet to look at the last book of the Pentateuch—Deuteronomy, and obtain its final witness of the numerical stamp upon it.

Deuteronomy is as plain as the other books. We

have in it, first of all, the rehearsal of Israel's journeyings through the wilderness,—of God's ways with
them, and of the conduct on their part which necessitated these ways. Then the divine commandments are
put before them, and the way of obedience shown to
be the way of blessing, as of disobedience the way of
curse. Finally, it is prophesied how the future would,
to their sorrow and shame, confirm all this, while
God would be as sovereign in their blessing in the
end as holy in the way by which he brings them into it.

Here the Pentateuch closes, then, and we shall have
no similar book to illustrate the two final numbers. For
Joshua is not a sixth book (in the sense we are considering), but a new *first*—the opening of a new series ;
neither does any book of Scripture go beyond a *fifth*.
The Pentateuchal structure, as we may by and by see,
is the structure of the whole Bible,—of the Old Testament and the New alike.

6.

We come now to the number 6. According to the
parallel of 5 and 7, it will consist of 4 *plus* 2, but its
arithmetical division would be 3 x 2. It is a number
which is thus, like 4, capable of true division.

Six days make up man's week of labor—a labor
which has come in through sin. This stamps his life,
which also has its limit—narrow and fixed by God.
Six speaks thus of divine limit imposed, of restraint
upon man's will, which breaks out against it and
submits, as the sea against its margin of sand, which
it cannot pass.

Thus, if 2 be taken here as the stamp of the enemy
and sin his work, the arithmetical division, which is

true *division*, speaks of God manifest in opposition to this—of His victory over it. But if 3 be taken as manifestation itself, not necessarily divine, then it may stand for the manifestation of the evil itself, which its end in due time brings about. On the other hand, if 3 stands (as we have seen it may) for fullness, then 6 may speak of the full development of evil, though always probably with this underlying thought of the divine control of it in spite of all.

The number of the beast, 666, whatever else it may have in it, would thus speak of the full development of evil in the very highest opposition to God; while also the stamp of vanity and weakness of the creature, limited and restrained by Him, would be only proportionately the more apparent.

In any case, the limitation, restraint, and perhaps judgment of evil seem to be inseparable from the number. Discipline would thus come under it.

This is but a meagre account, no doubt, and further research would assuredly enlarge our conceptions; yet it is a number which Scripture seems to avoid, if one may so say, and we shall have comparatively few examples of it in what is before us.

7.

Last of the series, we have the number 7, whose significance has been already noted. The division of 7 almost always is into 4 and 3, as also we have seen. The number of divine manifestation is added to the world-number,—God is made known in connection with the work of His hands : then He rests. Seven is thus the number of *perfect divine accomplishment*.

Thus the series of numbers is manifestly complete.

God is the beginning and end of it, the "First and with the last." There is room for nothing more. There is nothing that may not be resolved into what is contained herein. All higher numbers,—save one, which, as we have seen, is added to give confirmation, as it were, of the fact that the series is finished,—are but multiples of the lower ones, and as already said, gain their meaning from these which are (not merely arithmetically) their factors. We have seen 12 to be thus 4 x 3, and 10 to be a 5 x 2. Forty, again, the number of complete probation, is thus obviously only 4 x 10. There are few other of the larger numbers which seem to have any special prominence in Scripture.

Seven is the number which in its full sense speaks of the perfect accomplishment of the divine work. But we must not suppose that it is, any more than the others of the series, to be read only in this way. It seems indeed always to speak of perfection in some sense; but the sense is often a much lesser and lower one. Nor only so, it is occasionally used even in application to what is evil, as in the case of the man out of whom the unclean spirit had departed, but who returns with "seven other spirits more wicked than himself, and they enter in and dwell there." Now here, it seems to me that 6 is not used, as we might have expected, just because 6 implies, as we have seen, the control of the divine hand over the evil; and this, in such a warning as the Lord is giving, would not be in place. The man is given over to them; although, of course, there is, in another sense, and always, divine control.

The seven heads upon the apocalyptic beast have again a different meaning. They express only a *complete phase* of the beast's existence, which gives place to that under the *eighth* head, in which all the full height of spiritual evil is reached. Thus the 7 here is not the stamp of perfect evil, plainly.

This book of Revelation is full of sevens, as we must be all aware. The seven candlesticks, which are the seven churches, give us the light for the earth; *in responsibility*, a perfect testimony. The seven addresses give us the perfect judgment of how that responsibility has been discharged. The seven spirits before the throne represent the plenitude of the Spirit's energy. The seven seals and trumpets both terminate in the complete accomplishment of God's purposes as to the earth. In the seven vials, "the wrath of God" is expressly said to be "filled up." These will give us sufficient illustration of the use of the number 7, which is in general no very difficult one. Every application, indeed, requires careful consideration, and from this we shall never be released in studying Scripture. It is the labor in which assuredly there is profit.

Thus the numerical series ends, for of the number 8 all has been already said that need be said. As expressing (as in the first day of a new week) what is *new*, in contrast with the old, now passed away, it marks the former series as complete. It is the stamp of the *new* covenant, *new* creation, only characterizing them as that. It adds, therefore, no thought morally or spiritually; all this is summed up in the previous series.

We have, then, the series complete, however little

the interpretation may be.   Yet *true*, I believe it is, and while already there has been given some proof of this, it will be tested abundantly in that which lies before us.   Certainly it is of a nature to expose itself in the fullest way to testing.   We have yet to find also how the numerical division of Scripture works practically in bringing out its meaning; as only now are we furnished for this inquiry.   The practical test is the great one.   Is the metal gold, or a counterfeit? Yet if it be in Scripture, its genuineness and its profit are alike assured us.   "*All* Scripture . . . . *is* profitable.'' If God has been pleased to stamp all Scripture with this numerical stamp, how great must be the profit intended for us in it!

Now I propose, if the Lord enable me, to take up, in the lectures following this, the Bible as a whole, and to show how this numerical key opens to us its structure, the meaning of its individual books, and their relation to one another.   I desire to show how the seal of perfect inspiration is thus set upon every part,— that there is nothing in excess, nothing lacking, so that every stone in the building being in its place, filling exactly the place appointed it, its symmetry and beauty shall be apparent to every eye opened of God to see spiritually.   This is much to do assuredly.   If it be done, will not the numerical structure approve itself, not only as a *fact*, but one of immense importance?

But before we proceed to proof upon this larger scale, let us, for the remainder of this present lecture, attempt it upon a smaller one.   And let us take up some part sufficiently known to be grasped with some ease in its main features, then let us apply to it the law of Scripture which we believe we have discovered in it —that every part is marked with some number which conveys to us its real significance, and let us see what the result may be.

And for this purpose we will take up a passage which shall exhibit to us the whole series of numbers we have had in consideration,—a passage which divides into seven main parts, as well as whatever number of smaller parts. The Sermon on the Mount, familiar as it must be to all of us, will be in this way as suitable a passage perhaps as could be found.

In speaking of these divisions, let me remark that, in order that they may be clearer to us, and for this reason only, I shall call the largest portions of all, *divisions;* the portions of these, *parts;* and of these again, *sections.* When we have to go further than this, we shall speak in the same arbitrary way of *subdivisions*, and of *subsections.* This will have the advantage of enabling us without confusion to keep the rank of these various portions in our mind, and therefore I shall adhere to this language with scrupulous exactness.

The gospel of Matthew has for its theme what is only in it called the "kingdom of heaven."

The first division introduces the King Himself, in two parts: His title; and the testimony to Him rejected by the people, and His glory vailed because of their unbelief. This occupies the first two chapters.

The second division occupies chaps. iii.–vii. It treats of the "announcement of the kingdom," and divides into three parts. In the first, the King comes forth and receives the Father's acknowledgment at His anointing with the Holy Ghost. In the second part, we have the testimony of the King Himself. The third part occupies from chap. v.–vii., and here we have our subject—the Sermon on the Mount.

It is a true *third part*, treating as it does of the sanctification belonging to the kingdom, and this throughout.

The Sermon on the Mount divides into 7 sections, as already said, a number which stamps it with the perfection necessary to it as that which is the code of heaven's kingdom, from the lips of the Holy One of God.

The first section gives (v. 1–16) the beatitudes; which reveal in fact, the principles of the kingdom, as seen in the character of those who enter it. The blessings are pronounced upon them in three characters: *first* (1–9), as what they are personally, their righteousness, the kingdom controling and forming them, as chap. vi. 33; *secondly* (10–12), as persecuted by a world in opposition to them; *thirdly*, as salt amid the corruption, and light amid the darkness of the world.

The second section is a longer one, and has seven subdivisions. It occupies the rest of the chapter, and in it we find the law *confirmed*, expanded and supplemented. Observe, too, how there runs through the whole the contrast between what was said to them of old time and what *He* now says. In all of this, a second section is manifest.

The first subdivision (17–20) gives the maintenance of its *authority*, with the whole authority of the kingdom itself.

The second (21–26) begins the expansion of it with that of the commandment, "Thou shalt not kill;" forbidding the enmity of the heart in its least outflow, and establishing the law itself as the adversary to be reconciled by one against whom his brother thus has ought.

The third (27–32) goes to the heart and the root of lust there, while in the revision of the law of divorce it forbids one being the occasion of it in another.

The fourth (33–37) forbids oaths in recognition of the place of the creature before God, and of creature-weakness.

The fifth (38–42) treats of legal recompense on the principle of ver. 5, meekness, not resisting evil, an appeal and a submission, in fact, to divine government.

While the sixth (43–47) enjoins love to enemies— the truest and highest victory over evil, in imitation of God's own patient goodness toward such.

And the seventh (v. 48) closes with a plain injunction to *perfection*, even as our Father in heaven is perfect.

Thus to the end of this second section the numerical structure is clear and manifest, and points out the special features of every part. The closer the attention given to it the more manifest it will be.

The third section occupies the first eighteen verses of chap. vi. It treats of righteousness in the presence of the Father, who seeth in secret: practical righteousness, of course. (The Revised Version rightly reads this instead of "alms" in the first verse.)

This divides into three subdivisions—three different examples of what righteousness is, very different from any thing man would have given : first, alms, the expression of mercy, goodness undemanded save by the misery it relieves. This is the imitation in a creature of God's free bounty. Secondly, prayer, the expression of dependence, of the inferior place ; thirdly, fasting, the keeping under of the body, and bringing it into subjection—the expression of sanctification as led of the Spirit (Rom. viii. 12–14).

The fourth section fills the rest of the chapter. It gives the remedy for the cares and temptations of the world. First, in having one only place for heart and treasure ; secondly, in refusing divided service, the darkness of an evil eye ; thirdly, in the assurance of being under a Father's eye.

The first fourteen verses of the seventh chapter, as a fifth section, give *results in government*. First, of the measure you mete, which will be measured to you again ; secondly, of not dividing between holy and unclean ; thirdly, you must ask to receive, seek to find, knock that it may be opened, and a Father's love will give *good* gifts ; but fourthly, take care you do what you would have done ; and fifthly, only the strait gate and the narrow way lead to life.

The sixth section is a warning against false prophets —whose end shall be according to their works : a double exemplification of the number as it seems to me, for the false prophet is surely himself covered by it (vii. 15–23).

Finally, the seventh section puts the seal upon Christ's teachings : His perfect words are a rock-foundation for one that builds upon them ; when the final storms come, his building shall not be overthrown. This is the seal eternity will set upon Christ's word. Meanwhile, the authority of the Speaker shines through His decisive, inimitable sayings. This is the present seal: "He spake as One that had authority, and not as the scribes."

This is but the skeleton of a living and breathing reality. Still even a skeleton may exhibit something of a symmetry of structure which in fact we are now seeking to point out. Surely I have succeeded in showing that the numerical stamp is on this whole discourse of our Lord, and that it gives the real significance of the various parts. A closer examination would show this better, but it must suffice me for the present to have shown it.

And if this be shown as to these chapters of Matthew's gospel, then there is no shadow of reason for doubting that the numerical structure pervades all Scripture, from Genesis to Revelation. The chapters we have looked at have been chosen out of hundreds of others merely because they are a completely marked off subject, furnish examples of all the numbers, and are quite familiar, it is supposed, to all of us. They may be safely taken as illustrations of a pervading law; which, binding Scripture as it does together, we may challenge the keenest scepticism to dissolve its organic unity, or untie the knot of its perfect inspiration.

LECTURE IV

THE BIBLE BOOKS: THEIR ARRANGEMENT AND RELATIONSHIP

WE are now to take up the Bible as a whole, beloved brethren, to study the form in which it has come into our hands, and its parts, and the relation of these to each other and the whole. Is it a complete organic unity? Is there nothing defective, nothing redundant? There are other books mentioned in Scripture itself, as the book of Jasher, the book of the wars of the Lord, and others: are these books which perhaps have fallen out and are lost out of the canon? If so, can we recognize this? is there any gap apparent where their place should be? Is there any way of settling such questions?

Again, the Greek version of the Old Testament, the Septuagint, the version in common use in our Lord's time, and freely quoted by Himself and His apostles, adds not a few so-called apocryphal books to the canon, and some of these are pronounced by the Romish church to have really their place in it. Has the numerical system any thing to say to this?

And once more, there are in our New-Testament canon, books whose genuineness and authenticity have been in question, as, the epistle of Jude, and the second epistle of Peter: can we give any fresh light as to this? or whether the epistle to the Hebrews is the work of Paul, or of some Alexandrian, like Apollos?

Questions such as these are still asked, and although

few of them perhaps trouble us seriously to-day, yet
there are few also as to which a fresh and decisive
answer would not be welcome. Cannot the numerical
system, if it be really what is claimed for it, settle some
at least of these points? May we not expect as much
from it?

It is not too much to say that the numerical system
is able to settle them *all*, and fully settle them, so that
no reopening shall be possible. It is capable of showing the completeness of the Bible as a whole, the place
of every book, the relation of every book to the whole
and to each other. This may seem to be much to claim,
but if God be its author, who shall say that it is too
much? And this is what we are to begin the proof of
in the present lecture.

First of all, then, as to the number of the books; is
there any thing in this? I am not likely to forget
how, some years since, upon a country road, I asked
myself this question. The answer I got, you will, I
think, admit, was calculated to produce in me the
conviction that there is nothing in this line which is
not significant.

In the Old Testament, there are just thirty-six books:
in our present Bibles, indeed, thirty-nine; but all critics
are agreed that the three double books, Samuel, Kings,
and Chronicles, are in fact but each *one* book: the
Septuagint was the first version in which they were
divided, and from this it has crept into our common
Hebrew Bibles. But the Hebrew at first knew nothing
of it.

Thirty-six Old-Testament books, then: what should
we make of this? The number could be taken, of

course, as 6 x 6, and would be thus of no significance that I am aware of; but the most readily occurring division perhaps would be into 3 x 12, and here the numerals are full of meaning. Three is the divine number, the number of the Persons in the Godhead; 12, the number of divine government in the open form it took in Israel. What, then, more significant than this—"God in government"—as the characteristic of the thirty-six books of the law?

In the New Testament, on the other hand, there are twenty-seven books, and this is just the most perfect number that can be: it is the cube of 3,—3 x 3 x 3,—the only number beyond 3 itself into which the symbol of divine fullness and manifestation alone enters, and in its highest power. "God in government" is God hidden: clouds and darkness are round about Him; though His glory be seen, it is, as with Moses on the mount, His back, and not His face; but it is the glory of the gospel that it reveals Him, and in Christ we see His face. This the number 27 means,—God without a vail, God fully manifest; and what more significant and beautiful than this numerical stamp upon the twenty-seven books of the New Testament?

Take one book, then, away from either the Old Testament or the New, the significance is gone, the voice has died out; it is not any more as now a living voice that appeals to us. Add another book to either, the same result is found. Does not this, then, as plainly as simply declare to us that we have the full inspired canon (as to the number of books at least,) just as God designed it for us?

But we are only at the beginning of what the nu-

merals show. The two parts into which the Bible
divides we have already glanced at. The *first*, the Old
Testament, or Covenant, is thus marked as the
creation-, the *second*, the New Testament, as the
redemption-part. The Old Testament takes up man
in the flesh, addressing itself to one of the " families
of the earth," as such. A man was *born* of the seed
of Israel, not *new*-born. The New Testament addresses
itself to the saved—to those in Christ Jesus. This is
again the indication of a completely characteristic
difference.

We must look at the arrangement of the books before we can go further. And first, *have* we any
authoritative arrangement of the books? The question
may seem strange to not a few of us. A reader simply of the English Bible finds, in these days of printing and uniformity of copies, one invariable order of
books, which he naturally supposes, therefore, has been
from the beginning. He would be very likely to consider any interference with this an act of rashness and
an infringement upon the sacred character of the book.
On the other hand, the reader of the Hebrew Bible
finds an order different in many respects. The Septuagint has another, although in most respects similar to
the English one, which is derived from it. This, of
course, affects only the Old Testament. But in the
New Testament also the Greek copies show, as is well
known, many minor variations in order, although these
are confined to the epistles.

To return to the Old Testament, the Hebrew arrangement would seem to have the first claim to be
considered, the more so that we find its threefold divi-

sion into "Law, Prophets, and Writings," apparently recognized by our Lord Himself, in Luke xxiv. 44, as "the law of Moses, the prophets, and the psalms." This inverts the order, let it be noted, of our books, putting the prophets before the psalms. It would surely seem that so far we are bound, if the Lord Himself attach importance to the order, to the Hebrew arrangement.

Further than this, however, when we turn to the Hebrew, we seem to be confronted by a strangeness of the order which perplexes us. The simplicity of that in our ordinary Bibles seems strangely disturbed, and the last class of *Kethubim*, "writings," is made the receptacle for fragments torn unnaturally from their kindred books, and as unnaturally brought together.

And where are the rest of the historical books? They stand under the second head, as the "earlier prophets,"—the Jews claiming them to be written by prophets,—certain books, however, being cut off from them for the *Kethubim*, while the prophets proper,—or "*later* prophets," lose also two books; and the "writings" fall thus into three divisions: first, the Psalms, Proverbs, Job; secondly, the Song of Songs, Ruth, Lamentations, Ecclesiastes, Esther; thirdly, Daniel, Ezra, Nehemiah, and Chronicles.

Now this order, strange as it seems, might of course have deeper wisdom in it than we see. It would be mere rationalism at once to set it aside because of its apparent lack in this respect. But the question seems in place, Is this accepted as the order invariably? I quote an extract from Delitzsch on the book of Job, which will show how far this is from being the fact:—

" As the work of the Chokma [the didactic class], the book of Job stands, with the three other works belonging to this class of the Israelitish literature, among the Hagiographa, which are called in Hebrew simply *Kethubim*. Thus, by the side of the Law and the Prophets, the third division of the canon is styled, in which are included all those writings belonging neither to the province of prophetic history nor prophetic declaration. Among the Hagiographa are writings even of a prophetic character, as Psalms and Daniel, but their writers are not properly *prophets*. At present, Lamentations stands among them; *but this is not its original place, as also Ruth appears to have stood originally between Judges and Samuel.* Both Lamentations and Ruth are placed among Hagiographa, that there the five so-called *Megilloth*, or scrolls, may stand together: the Song of Songs, the feast-book of the eighth passover-day; Ruth that of the second Shabuoth-day; Lamentations, that of the ninth of Ab; Ecclesiastes, that of the eighth Tabernacle-day; Esther, that of Purim. . . . . The position which [the book of Job] occupies is, moreover, a very shifting one. In the Alexandrine canon, Chronicles, Ezra, Nehemiah, Tobit, Judith, Esther, follow the four books of the Kings. The historical books, therefore, stand, from the earliest to the latest, side by side; then begins with Job, Psalms, Proverbs, a new row, opened with these three in stricter sense poetical books. Then Melito of Sardis, in the second century, places Chronicles with the books of the Kings, but arranges immediately after them the non-historical Hagiographa in the following order: Psalms, Proverbs, Ecclesiastes, Canticles, Job. Here, the Solomonic writings are joined to the Davidic psalter, and the anonymous book of Job stands last. In our editions of the Bible, the Hagiographa division begins with Psalms, Proverbs, Job (the succession peculiar to MSS. of the German class): in the Talmud, with Ruth, Psalms, Job, Proverbs; in the Masora, and in MSS. of the Spanish class, with Chronicles, Psalms, Job, Proverbs. All these modes of arrangement are well considered."

Perhaps; but the only thing they leave plain is that the later arrangement of books differs from the earlier, that at any time perhaps arrangements differed; that that of the "five rolls" is simply a more or less recent one for liturgical purposes; and that we have no recognized *divine* one at all, save only that of the Law, the Prophets, and the Psalms, which the Lord recognized in the last chapter of Luke.

We are compelled, therefore, to examine for ourselves if there be any arrangement that we can recognize as divine at all, for a mere human one is not what we are seeking or would satisfy us in any respect. And here we will first of all look for what would seem a *natural* arrangement, and then see what, if any thing, the numerical system may have to say to it.

And undoubtedly what would *seem* most natural, in view of the one limitation which Scripture itself has imposed on us, would be in the main what we have in our Bibles, only reversing the order of the poetical and prophetic books. The historical books would thus stand first, in two divisions,—the Pentateuch, or Law, and the rest from Joshua. Here, the chronological order would apparently be the necessary one, with per, haps an exception in the case of Chronicles, which is a rehearsal of the history with a special purpose. Then we should have the Prophets, larger and smaller. Finally, the five poetical books.

Now what struck me as I looked at these four divisions, could not but inspire me with hope that here was indeed something like a divine arrangement. *Each of these divisions falls easily into five parts;* and upon looking similarly at the New Testament, it too seemed to fall also into five parts. *Five Pentateuchs make up the whole Bible!*

This was indeed to me an illuminating discovery. Was, then, that Pentateuch of Moses, so dishonored by the latter-day generation of critics, the basis of the structure of all Scripture? If this were so then, as surely as the foundation must be before the super-structure, so surely must these five books of the law have preceded all that was built upon them. These books, then, are an organic unity, and as such give form to all Scripture!

But let us see if it is so. The five books of Moses themselves, as the first Pentateuch, we need not of course discuss. The second division of historical books would give us,—

1. Joshua.
2. Judges; with which the little book of Ruth joins as a natural supplement. It is a story of the same times.
3. We have Samuel and Kings, which give us the kingdom in Israel from first to last.
4. The books of the captivity, three in number,— Ezra, Nehemiah, Esther.

5. Chronicles, a résumé of the history of the kingdom, with a special moral purpose.

Here is a division, a least, which none can deny to be natural. As to the order, the place of Chronicles is the only one that can be disputed, and this question we can afford for the present to leave. Otherwise, it will be admitted to be *natural*.

We may go on, then, to the Prophets. Here we have,—

1. Isaiah.
2. Jeremiah, with its supplement, Lamentations.
3. Ezekiel.
4. Daniel.
5. The Minor Prophets, twelve in number.

The order in our Bibles is here undisturbed. The only question that can arise as to naturalness is as to the classing the twelve minor prophets together as one division. For our purpose at present it is enough to say that the Jews seem always to have so classed them, and Melito of Sardis expressly calls them *monobiblos*— one book. The reason for this has been indeed said to be, lest on account of their size any one might be lost. But this on the face of it seems mere supposition, and it may be we can find, as we proceed, a better reason.

The fourth division needs no reasoning or explanation. It consists of but just five books. I put them in their true order, as I believe it, and hope afterward to give the ground of it. They are,—

1. Psalms.
2. Job.
3. Song of Songs.
4. Ecclesiastes.
5. Proverbs.

Passing to the New Testament, some have supposed a natural division would be into *three* parts,—the Historical books, Epistles, and Revelation. As to the form of writing, this is natural enough; but the subjects suggest a further division. For the Gospels claim surely to be distinguished from the Acts; while the Pauline epistles are equally distinguishable from those of the other inspired writers. In this case, we have again our five divisions.

If this were all, it would be a noticeable fact, but an unsatisfying one. Our minds necessarily ask, Why is it? and they are intended—may we not say?—to ask this. If God has so written His Word, it is *reverence* to ask, Is there not meaning in it? We may be sure there is. Shall He who has forbidden "idle words" do Himself an idle thing? No, surely. But we it is who wrong Him by our indifference and unbelief. "Said I not unto thee, that if thou wouldst *believe*, thou shouldst see the glory of God?" has manifold application. Let us now apply the test of which we have spoken, and see if the appearance of numerical structure we have found in this division of the books of Scripture be more than an appearance,—if these Pentateuchs in form be not Pentateuchs in spirit also,— and what else God may in His grace disclose to us, as we follow in this track.

If, then, the Pentateuch be the basis of the structure of Scripture, can we perhaps find any reason in this? The number 5, which this stamps upon it, should have in some way a spiritual significance corresponding in Scripture as a whole, if the numerical structure be indeed a reality. In the Pentateuch itself also we should find first of all this correspondence also, if it be really the fundamental form, as we have suggested. The form is only the fitting clothing of the spirit, and without the spirit the body is dead.

Five we have seen to speak of man exercised and responsible under the government of God; and this responsible creature, lost in his responsibilty, this soul exercised with so many questions, in a path darkened by sorrow and sin,—is he about whom nevertheless all God's infinite wisdom is employed, over whom His tender love is pouring itself out. The five books of the Pentateuch are just the connected picture of man in his whole course on earth—as the forlorn and wretched creature indeed that sin has made him, but this as the back-ground upon which to display the divine mercies to him. Thus Genesis begins the account with the story of the new life received from God, in its varied aspects and stages of development. Exodus then narrates his redemption; Leviticus details the holiness which suits and is demanded by his new relationship. Now he is qualified for a walk through the world, and this is the reason of the apparent descent in the character of the truth which Numbers next shows. Life, salvation, and the knowledge of God in the sanctuary are all needed in order to a walk with God thus; and in Numbers, the virtues of Christ's priesthood are made good to us, and His tender sympathy and care. Deuteronomy completes the picture with the full recital of God's ways with us and ours with Him, as the judgment-seat of Christ will make us realize them,—lessons of imperishable wisdom, which will be gathered up for us and made our own; not lost, but gained forever, when eternity opens for us its doors.

Thus the Pentateuch rounds off its significant series with the survey of the ground traversed, and the victories won; *His* victories, at all events, for us, oftentimes against ourselves; and we see how the jewels of divine grace and glory are strung upon the thread of human need and sorrow and sin. How sympathetic, how practical, how *human* is Scripture! How little are its truths conformed to theological systems! how constantly are they employed in meeting and ministering to the need of man! The most formal treatise, if I may so say, is the epistle to the Romans, and *that* is what has directly to do with the first necessities of the soul. The number 5 is stamped on all. The human thread runs through all. The Pentateuch is still and ever the basis of structure,—the architectural model of the whole.

The Bible is a Pentateuch of Pentateuchs; and the division into Old and New Testaments does not affect this; indeed brings it out more clearly for as 5 is a 4 + 1, so the Old Testament contains four Pentateuchs; the New, one. And the meaning corresponds throughout.

And why *four* Pentateuchs in the Old Testament? Evidently because 4 is the *world*-number, and the number which speaks of *trial*. Here, let us separate a little these connected thoughts, and view the Old Testament in two different aspects of it.

First, then, it is the earthly part of revelation, as the New Testament is the heavenly part. It is to the earthly people that it is addressed; it is an earthly outlook that is given in its widest scope of prophecy. No where does the law even conditionally promise a heavenly portion, but an earthly one. "The way into the holiest of all"—and that is, in type, heaven—"was not yet made manifest." "The heaven, even the heavens," says the Psalmist, "are the Lord's,"—or, as the Revised Version puts it better now, "The heavens are the heavens of the Lord; the *earth* hath he given to the children of men."

Thus, if the book of Revelation be compared with the greatest of Old-Testament prophets, you will find that in its view of the future it leaves out all those earthly promises upon which Isaiah and Ezekiel and others dilate, while it supplements them with a vision of the *heavenly* Jerusalem, and the reign of the heavenly saints.

But there is another meaning to this number 4 also, as it speaks of trial, probation. The Old-Testament books are those which take up those ages of probation at the end of which Christ came. To quote again the Revised Version, "Now once in the end of the ages hath He been manifested to put away sin by the sacrifice of Himself" (Heb. ix. 26). The character of these "ages" is elsewhere expressed: "When we were yet without strength, in due time Christ died for the ungodly" (Rom. v. 6). This is what the law, the great instrument of probation, manifested. This was the schoolmaster's lesson for those times. Hence, 4 x 5,—four Pentateuchs—once more give just expression to the character of the Old-Testament books.

And this unites singularly with the voice of chronology here, as I have elsewhere pointed out. The voices of chronologists are indeed so perplexingly at variance that it may be hard to say what is the voice of chronology at all. I pretend to no ability whatever to settle such questions, but simply taking up that which is to be found in our common Bibles, and taking from it, as we are said to be entitled to do, the odd four years, we find the Lord's birth falling on the four thousandth year of the world. A little knowledge of the significance of numbers, and of the characteristic of the previous ages as probational ones, makes that a very interesting date indeed. Four thousand years are, of course, *forty centuries*. Forty is the well-known symbol of probation in the fullest way. Israel had their forty years of trial in the wilderness, the Lord His forty days; Esau was forty years old when he married two Canaanitish wives, and stamped himself fully as the "profane person" which his renunciation of the birth-right had before indicated him to be.

The world's probation lasted forty *centuries*. But why this last factor?—why centuries?

The century is 10 x 10, the measure of responsibility once more, intensified, as this self-multiplication shows.

It was the term of Abraham's age when he "considered not his body now dead, when he was about a hundred years old, neither the deadness of Sarah's womb," and God fulfilled to him the promise so long delayed in the birth of Isaac. It cannot but appear, then, to stamp with accuracy and with significance the common reckoning, to find, when man was discovered dead, the true Isaac born according to it in the fortieth century of the world—the four thousandth year.

Four Pentateuchs, then, fill up the Old Testament.

Let us now see the significance of each of these in its place in the series.

First, the *books of the Law*. This bears the numerical stamp undoubtedly. The supremacy of God is what the law, of course, affirms.

The second division gives the *Covenant-History*. It is a history, alas! of sin and discord and division while also of divine deliverances, until even God's patience is at an end, and the people become Lo-Ammi (not My people). Even then, the return of a remnant is permitted, though under the Persian yoke, to repeat their old history on a smaller scale. The second book of this section, Judges, is morally the epitome of the whole of it.

The third division is that of the *Prophets;* and here we are brought, as in the sanctuary, face to face with God. "Thus saith the Lord" is the constant formula of the prophets, for *prophecy* is one speaking for another. Thus sanctification also is the great theme of the prophets, and not merely the prediction of the future, in which they see indeed this sanctification accomplished, and the glory of God at last fully revealed.

Finally, the fourth division is a peculiar one; it is undoubtedly that which especially speaks of the world as the place of trial for man, and the sorrows which are his lot in it; while all these books are, as in the five books of the Psalms, prominently marked with the number 5, which speaks of his exercises of heart amid these trials, so sure to be connected with them. (This number 5, as it is a 4 and 1, will naturally approach 4 in character; and so it does.) These books are thus pre-eminently the human voice in Scripture, in which all the dark and difficult problems of life find utterance.

We have thus the divisions marked, however, briefly; but it yet remains to establish, as to four of them, their real Pentateuchal significance. We shall have but room in this lecture to take up one of them, that which I have called the "Covenant-History," as being, in fact, the history of the people of God in relation to that legal covenant which the first division saw established with them at Mount Sinai. Let us now, then, proceed to this.

1. *Joshua.*

The first part here is the book of Joshua; or, "Jehovah the Saviour." It treats, as the foundation of all the rest, of the conquest of the land of promise, and their establishment in it, spite of the opposition of their enemies, by the sovereign power of God. It fills its numerical place as being thus the fulfillment, by almighty power, of the counsels of electing love toward them. The sovereignty of God is strongly affirmed in the very first chapter; the law being His expressed will, subjection to it strength and victory. By His power alone Jordan is cut off below and its streams held back above, the ark of His strength being in the river. By His power alone the walls of Jericho fall down. At Ai they are smitten for disobedience and independency of Him; this judged, the career of conquest rolls on with a flood tide, until, when only the middle of the book is reached, the whole power of the enemy is smitten before them, "and the land rested from war."

The power of the enemy is here prominent, for we are in the second division of the Old Testament; but it is for the most part external only, and Jehovah is their Saviour from it.

In one thing only do we miss in Joshua the general character of the Genesis-books, and that is with regard to the largeness of view which has given Genesis itself the title of "The seed-plot of the Bible." But this probably results only from our lack of knowledge. Quite one half of the book is typically almost closed to us, and yet here what a field presents itself for inquiry! The division of Canaan among the twelve tribes, how much it ought to speak to us of our inheritance beyond death! Oh, for faith so to go over and take possession of it, that the list of now almost barren names may reveal the beauty of a land "which is the glory of all lands," upon which the eyes of the Lord are continually"! *Our* eyes for all this beauty, where are they.*

2. *Judges.*

The second part, as we have seen, is composed of two books, both of which may be comprised under the common title of "Judges," as belonging to the same historical period, a period in sad contrast to that of the previous book. If Gilgal, which the angel of the Lord now leaves, and where the reproach of Egypt was rolled off, characterizes the times of Joshua, Bochim, or "Weepers," to which he comes, no less characterizes the times of the Judges. when the reproach of Egypt—

---

* I leave this as first written. I am thankful to be able to refer to the Numerical Bible in proof of how much, through the goodness of God, the numerical structure has since opened this out; and what a proof it has given of the value of this as a key to interpretation.

of servitude—has more than returned. The book before us speaks alike of sin and its terrible fruit in
Israel, although the second, as a sort of gospel-supplement to the first, is made to show us especially the
help laid upon One that is mighty, and Him "in whom
might is," as Boaz' name signifies. This is a secret
for the ear of faith, however ; the general history is in
the book of Judges.

1. Judges, as the first book here, reveals its character in that one word,—"independence." As heading
the second part of the historical books, it speaks of
the power of the enemy, of division in Israel, of captivity, alternating, however, through the goodness of
God toward them, with wonderful deliverances, in
which He again and again appears as their Saviour-
God. The mode of their deliverance—by judges who
judge the people for God—agrees, of course, with the
root of the evil to be met. "The judges," says Keil,
"were men who procured justice, or right, for the people of Israel, not only by delivering them out of the
power of the foes, but also by administering the laws
and rights of the Lord (chap. ii. 16–19.) *Judging* in
this sense was different from the administration of civil
jurisprudence, and included the idea of government
such as would be expected from a king."

The character of Judges is, then, just that which
should be found in the first book of a second part.

2. The place of Ruth we have seen to be a disputed
one, and, among the Jews in general, to be among the
Kethubim. Its place in the Septuagint, and among
the Hellenistic Jews, as Josephus and others, is referred by Keil to their "freer tendencies" as to inspi-

ration, such as made them intersperse the canonical with apocryphal books. Yet Keil admits that its position among the five *megilloth* "is connected with the liturgical use in the synagogue," while in the Talmud it is placed before the Psalms. This does not look as if the most orthodox Jews had any idea of any very specific divine order. Keil admits also, what indeed is evident, that "so far as its *contents* are concerned, it has its proper place between the book of Judges and those of Samuel."

It is evident also that in all the characters of the fourth division of the Old Testament it is deficient, and could only be classed with the book of Psalms (!) by some such negative and hypothetical mark as that it was not written by a prophet. On the other hand, that the Spirit of prophecy has dictated every thing in Ruth those will be assured who see in Boaz the picture of the true Kinsman-Redeemer of His people, whether Jew or Gentile. For, as the apostle argues, the Jew also must be saved like the Gentile, upon the ground of pure grace, so that Ruth may typify these as well as those.

That Ruth thus stands as a gospel-supplement to the ruin of man as Judges exhibits it appears clear from its connection both backward and forward also. And let us look at this briefly here.

To go back, then, to Joshua. The reference in Eph. vi. to the warfare with flesh and blood in Canaan, as contrasting it with our conflict "with principalities, and powers, with the rulers of the darkness of this world, with spiritual hosts of wickedness in the heavenly places" (as the Revised Version rightly puts it now), is an illumination of the book of Joshua. For that Canaan typifies these heavenly places, which are for faith our present inheritance, is recognized by Christians generally. Joshua's name is exactly that of our so much greater Leader; and here we have the *present* conflict of faith, in which the devil resists our taking possession of the good land that belongs to us.

The land is ours, fruit of our Jesus' victory; but alas! our failure—the failure of the whole professing church to realize possession is as evident. The book of Judges typifies thus the break-down of the heavenly people: failures and revivals, captivities and deliverances,—this has been the history of christendom nearly from the beginning. The *end*, as to earthly history, is in failure, a collapse of the Christian as of the Jewish dispensation.

Now here comes in the book of Ruth, which exhibits (how beautifully!) the Kinsman-Redeemer as Him in whom alone is strength. The Gentile heavenly, as the Jewish earthly, bride must creep to His feet, and claim Him in lowliness, as debtors only to His grace. Thus is He, then, for them.

The way is then open for the book of Samuel—for David and the kingdom.

3. *The Books of the Kings.*

The third part is composed likewise of two books, for we have seen that Samuel and Kings are but one book each. The connection between these, and their distinction from all others, is plain enough. They are both books of the Kings, and the title of Samuel for the first seems really a misnomer. From the very beginning, in Hannah's song of praise, the anointed king is in view. The opening shows the priesthood, as a link between God and the people, morally gone. Soon the ark of the covenant is actually gone; and although it could not remain in the Philistines' land, and quickly returns to within the Israelitish limits, yet to the people themselves it scarcely can be said to return till David brings it to Zion.

Thus this third part is a resurrection-period; and the prophet at first becomes the spiritual link between God and the people. When the kingdom is afterward divided, and Israel is following Baal or the golden calves, then the prophet is again an extraordinary link while the patience of God holds out toward them. Thus the books of the Kings speak more of the prophet than all the rest of the historic books together. This is clearly a numerical mark, therefore.

But the prophet is, as I have said, the introduction to the king, and the king is of course the prominent feature in these books. This seems, on the other hand, a difficulty. But it is more than relieved, I think, by considerations to which I have been led but recently.

We have seen that the book of Samuel opens with the ruin of the priesthood, and that the ark, though soon returning out of the enemies' land, is not by this restored to its former position. In the words of the seventy-eighth psalm, "He forsook the tabernacle of Shiloh, the tent which He pitched among men." To that tabernacle He *never returns*. The ark remains at Kirjath-jearim, in the house of Abinadab, all the time of Samuel and of Saul. The tabernacle we find afterward removed to Gibeon, but it is empty; nor is the ark "inquired at in the days of Saul" (1 Chron. xiii. 3).

It is this that in the hundred and thirty-second psalm burdens the soul of David: "Surely I will not come into the tabernacle of my house, nor climb up into my bed; I will not give sleep to my eyes, nor slumber to my eyelids, until I find out a place for the Lord, a habitation for the mighty God of Jacob." The ark is brought to Zion, and God says, "This is My rest forever; here will I dwell, for I have desired it." But the temple is built only by Solomon: not the man of war, but the prince of peace must build it.

And in all this, a greater than David or Solomon is to be seen. It is Christ who alone can give to God a final dwelling-place among men: "Behold the Man whose name is The Branch; and He shall grow up out of His place, and He shall build the temple of the Lord, even He shall build the temple of the Lord; and He shall bear the glory, and shall sit and rule upon His throne; and He shall be a priest upon His throne: and the council of peace shall be between them both" (Zech. vi. 12, 13).

Thus behind the kingship in Israel there is this greater question of the dwelling of God with men. The king was necessary to this. Sovereign power must unite with priestly intercession, and a David must put down opposition, in order for a Solomon to reign in peace and build the temple of the Lord. For this, the whole book of Samuel is a preparation; the book of Kings shows it a completed thing. But these are only shadows of the true, therefore they pass. The sabbatic rest is broken up again by sin. The kingdom is divided, the temple desecrated, and the nation finally dispersed.

He is not yet come who unites the kingship and the priesthood in His own person. David, as a shadow, may wear the ephod, and order the worship, and provide the song; but the true Priest must be the risen One: the almond-rod with its fruit out of death must be His type. King and priest fall asunder therefore; the gleam of light passes away: the glory leaves the temple on earth, and the characteristic of the next books is that God is the "God of heaven." The kingdoms of the earth are given to the Gentile.

This is an account too brief and shallow, yet it should make plain that the great question in the books before us is that of the sanctuary of God on earth. And this makes them a most suited third section. Of these,—

(1) Samuel, as the first book, speaks of the introductory tabernacle-period;—

(2) Kings, of the temple completed, and a reign of glory and peace; but then of sin, of service divided with false gods, of division in the kingdom, henceforth in intestine strife, of deliverances also indeed, and the testimony of the prophets raised up, but still of constant and worse departure, until the divided kingdom falls a prey to its enemies.

4. *The Books of the Captivity.*

The times of the Gentiles are now begun; the glory of God is in Jerusalem no more, and God is the God of heaven. This gives the books of the captivity, with all their diversity, a sorrowful unity, and separates them from the other historical books. This is the Numbers part of the historical books—what God calls, in Ezek. xx. 35, "The wilderness of the peoples," in which He pleads with Israel, and causes them to pass under the rod. This condition is, of course, not ended, for the times of the Gentiles are not.

The fourth division speaks, then, of this time of trial; yet it has three books, while each of the two before it have but two. For while the blessing before enjoyed was only a shadow of the true, final one, their sorrow leads to that final one itself, when (as the passage in Ezekiel goes on to say,) "Ye shall know that I am the Lord." We shall find among the Minor Prophets a similar fourth section in the prophets of this very period, in which there are likewise three books, of which Haggai and Zechariah undoubtedly correspond with Ezra and Nehemiah, while Malachi, less obviously, but still really, corresponds with Esther.

(1) First, then, of these books comes Ezra, in which we have the return of a remnant to Jerusalem, and the restoration of the temple there. But there is now no Urim and Thummim, no ark, no glory: the temple is empty,—so that this is not a third division as before, but a *first;* for its true significance is *God's sovereignty*, which sways the kings of the earth, and in which He fulfils the promise of return after seventy years; and the subjection of the remnant to this sovereign God as His worshipers.

(2) Nehemiah, then, gives to this remnant so returned (as his name imports) the "comfort of the Lord." The walls of the city are built, and their de-

liverance from their enemies accomplished. "As the hills stand round about Jerusalem, so the Lord standeth round about His people."

(3) The book of Esther gives us (in what is of course only an anticipation of it) the manifestation of God in the resurrection of the people; the Jewish bride displacing the Gentile, and the Jewish Mordecai, as another Joseph, exalted to the power of the throne; the enemies of Israel subdued under them.

My object here being simply to show in the place of these books the reality of the numerical structure, this meagre outline may be yet sufficient. The filling in must be sought elsewhere.

5. *Chronicles.*

Finally, we have, as the Deuteronomy of this division, the book of Chronicles; and it should be easily apparent that it fills, in fact, this place. As Deuteronomy was a rehearsal of Israel's ways with God in the wilderness, so is Chronicles of the history of the Kings. And as the *divine* ways shine out in Deuteronomy, so do they in the book before us. The purpose of enforcing obedience as the way of blessing is most evident. Thus Keil says,—

"Now from these and other descriptions of the part the Levites played in events, and the share they took in assisting the efforts of pious kings to revivify and maintain the temple worship, the conclusion has been rightly drawn that the chronicler describes with special interest the fostering of the Levite worship according to the precepts of the law of Moses, and holds it up to his contemporaries for earnest imitation; yet . . . .

the chronicler does not desire to bring honor to the Levites and to the temple worship: his object is rather to draw from the history of the kingship in Israel a proof that faithful adherence to the covenant which the Lord had made with Israel brings happiness and blessing; the forsaking of it, on the contrary, insures ruin and a curse."

The book of Chronicles is thus very exactly the Deuteronomy of the covenant-history, and with this brief statement our review of the historical books must for the present close.

LECTURE V

The Books of the Prophets

WE are now to take up the books of the prophets, the third division of the Old Testament, and that in which we are most of all brought face to face with God Himself. The vail is of course not yet removed; yet as more and more the condition of the people was discovered hopeless, and even as judgment more and more, stroke upon stroke, fell upon them, to faith God began to speak with increasing plainness. That the just shall live by faith was witnessed by a prophet, and how full and plain is Isaiah as to the work and glory of Christ! We are surely in the sanctuary in this third division, and the holiness of the place makes itself apparent at every step.

Yet the prophets are little studied, little known; and when studied, it is more as *predictions* than to realize their spiritual meaning: thus, again, they have fallen with many into a disrepute sadly dishonoring to Him who speaks in them more undisguisedly than elsewhere in the Old Testament. "Surely the Lord God will do nothing," says Amos, "but He revealeth it unto His servants the prophets."

We shall not be able to do more than glance at some of their distinctive features at the present time; and for my own part, I realize more what hidden treasures there must be in them than can pretend to have found them. Still, even the briefest outline may invite research, and my purpose is now to show what may be without much difficulty shown, that here also we find that numerical structure which we have been tracing elsewhere.

But let us notice, before we take this up, what cannot but have interest for us as awakening our attention at least to the minute things of Scripture, that of the greater prophets the names singularly agree with the position necessitated by the times in which they wrote. Thus Isaiah and Jeremiah prophesied in the period when the people were yet the people of the Lord, and Jah, or Jehovah, the covenant-title, is compounded with their names. The one means "The Salvation of Jehovah;" the other, "Jehovah shall establish." The two others prophesied after the captivity had begun, and *their* names are compounded with that of God simply. Ezeki*el*, "God shall strengthen;" and Dani*el*, "God my Judge."

There is indeed among the prophets of the captivity, one whose name is also compounded with Jehovah,— Zechariah, "Jehovah hath remembered;" but it seems to me that this is only an apparent contradiction: for Zechariah seems only exceptionally to address himself to the present, and to be wholly occupied with that which is to come; and perhaps his very name points out this. It is at least singular to find, when we open the gospel of Luke, another Zechariah, whose name, with that of his wife Elizabeth, ("The oath of God,') is clearly significant of *covenant owned:* "The Lord"— Jehovah—"*hath remembered* His holy covenant, *the oath which He sware* to our father Abraham." Is this merely a casual, or a designed coincidence? It was the utterance of one "filled with the Holy Ghost."

But to come to our subject:—

1. *Isaiah*—

is, there need be no doubt, the Genesis of the Prophets. Even that which may seem at first sight against it is in fact an evidence of it, namely, the exceeding largeness of the scope of his prophecy, which seems to concentrate all lines of truth and blessing. Thus he is called the "evangelical prophet," and the "prophet of salvation," and a glance at a concordance will show how much he uses the very words, "salvation," "Saviour," "redemption," "Redeemer." But so, with almost more appropriateness might he be called the prophet of sanctification, so full is he of "holiness," and of the "Holy One." But this is the fulness of one who is eminently the prophet of the divine counsels. "Counsel" and "purpose" are common words also with him:—"I have purposed;" "The Lord of Hosts hath purposed;" "My purpose shall stand, and I will do all My pleasure;" "The counsel of the Lord;" "Which is wonderful in counsel;" "Thy counsels of old are faithfulness and truth."

So His omniscience is dwelt upon:—"New things do I declare: before they spring forth I tell you of them." "Who as I shall call and shall declare it and set it in order for Me, since I appointed the ancient people? and the things that are coming and shall come, let them show them unto them." "Who hath declared this from ancient time? who hath told it from that time? have not I the Lord?" "I have declared the former things from the beginning; and they went forth out of My mouth, and I showed them; I did them suddenly, and they came to pass." "Declaring the end from the beginning, and from ancient times the things that are not yet done."

He chooses and calls :—Israel are, again and again, "My elect;" "My chosen;" "Jacob, whom I have chosen;" "My servant, whom I have chosen;" "Israel, whom I have chosen." "I the Lord have called thee;" "I have called thee by thy name;" "Yea, I have called him;" "I have called him alone;" "When I call unto them, they stand up together."

The last passage is an assertion of creative power, and this too is again and again dwelt on :—"The everlasting God, the Lord, the Creator of the ends of the earth;" "He that created the heavens;" "The Lord that created thee;" "The Creator of Israel;" "I make light and create darkness: I make peace and create evil;" "I create new heavens and a new earth;" "The Lord that made thee;" "The Lord that maketh all things."

Thus He is the one only God: "Who hath directed the Spirit of the Lord, or being His counselor hath taught Him?" "To whom, then, will ye liken God?" "To whom, then, will ye liken Me, or shall I be equal?" "I the Lord, the First, and with the last," "I am the Lord, that is My name, and My glory will I not give to another;" "I am the First, and I am the Last, and beside Me there is no God;" "Is there a God beside Me? yea, there is no God;" "That stretcheth forth the heavens alone, that spreadeth forth the earth by Myself."

These are only a part of the testimonies that might be collected, but surely there is no need to multiply them further. In others of the prophets no doubt some similar passages may be found, but Isaiah is the home of such expressions, and some are peculiar to it. Ezekiel uses the word "create" three times; Jeremiah, Amos, Malachi, once each; and these are all the occurrences in the Prophets. The *making* of the heavens and earth is ascribed to or claimed by God five times in Jeremiah; of the sea and the dry land, once in Jonah; of *one* woman for the man, once in Malachi; and Jeremiah and Hosea once speak of God as the "Maker." In Isaiah, this word alone is used in such connections fifteen times. "Forming" is ascribed to God similarly in Jeremiah, six times; in Amos, twice; in Zechariah, once. Isaiah uses it |eighteen times.

The "First and the Last," or "with the last," is found three times in Isaiah, and never elsewhere.

I mention these things simply to meet the thought that probably others of the prophets might yield similar results if searched for them. It is not at all so. Examination only demonstrates the characteristic difference more and more. He is the prophet of the divine supremacy, counsel and sovereign will; his prophecies are the Genesis of the Prophets.

2. *Jeremiah.*

There is more difficulty in showing Jeremiah to be the Exodus; and indeed we must notice all through Scripture that every book has its *individuality;* no one is a mere repetition of another. And in these comparisons which we are making, we shall find a wide variety under every resemblance. It is said no two leaves can be found upon a tree which exactly resemble one another. And God is everywhere the same God.

The first thing we may notice in Jeremiah is the prominence of the person of the prophet, and how much in various ways he seems to typify the Lord. This is noticed by commentators generally, while unbelievers of various kinds have taken him as the representative of the Servant of the Lord in Isaiah's wondrous picture of the Messiah (Is. liii).

Undoubtedly, of all the prophets he is the man of sorrows, rejected as he is by his personal intimates and by the nation at large, while bearing in his soul their burdens, and feeling the broken bonds of relationship between Jehovah and His chosen nation. In this spirit he becomes the mediator between them, although here the contrast between type and Antitype cannot but come out. It is this intense sorrow which spreads itself over the brightness we should expect in a prophetic Exodus. The living affection of the Spirit of Christ manifests itself yet in this sorrow.

And there are passages in which the storm clears away, and the sun shines brightly out. "The Lord our Righteousness" is found twice in Jeremiah, and found no where else; although Isaiah has more than once a parallel thought. But the "new covenant" is the explicit announcement of Jeremiah only, and when we know that the "new testament" is but this "new covenant," and how Paul glories in being a "minister of the new covenant," then he does indeed become the prophet above all others of the present grace. The breaking of the legal tie between Jehovah and Israel, while it is the effect and judgment of their sins, is made, in the wondrous goodness of God, the occasion of setting aside the law "for the weakness and unprofitableness thereof, for the law made nothing perfect." "For if that first covenant had been faultless," says the apostle. "then should no place have been sought for the second ; for finding fault with them, He saith, Behold, the days come, saith the Lord, when I will make a new covenant . . . In that He saith, 'a new covenant,' He hath made the first old."

How important, then, is this word by Jeremiah! The very ruin and break-up of existing things in the midst of which he moves brings him there where he can contemplate clearly the new grace that is to follow. No prophet, then, takes so fully, after all, the Exodus-place as he.

(2) *Lamentations* is of course the supplement to Jeremiah ; and not a supplement of joy, but a strain of sorrow, as its title indicates, over the desolate city. I know no characteristics by which to separate it from the book of the prophet itself, except that it is not a prophecy but a lament.

But having in the outset of these lectures referred to its peculiar alphabetic structure, it may be now in place to show briefly how here also the structure corresponds with its inner meaning.

The five chapters we have seen to have each the alphabet running through them, except the fifth, which still retains, however, the twenty-two verses. The *third* chapter contains a triple alphabet and sixty-six verses.

The first chapter speaks of the solitariness and desolation of the city, gone into captivity, and owns it to be from God's hand in righteousness for their sin.

It is God who has done this, and the soul of the people, personated by the prophet, humbles itself before Him.

In the second part, it is the breach of relationship especially: God is turned to be as an enemy to that which was His own; it is destruction more than desolation, and while the words of the prophets have been but false burdens, He has but fulfilled His own word.

In the third part, it is Jehovah Himself that is before the soul: the bitterness is in its being from *Jehovah*. Yet here the burdened one begins to realize what is in Jehovah for him, and Himself is still his portion. The sorrow is discipline, and it is good to bear the yoke; while out of it all at last comes revival and blessing and the overthrow of enemies. This chapter of Lamentations we find to be (though the sanctuary be desolate) a sanctuary-psalm. Jehovah Himself is this.

The fourth chapter compares the former and the present estate, and sees the decline which has ended in ruin. Yet let not the enemy rejoice, for their punishment is at hand; while the punishment of His people will find an end yet with God.

Then the last chapter closes with their putting before Him the long catalogue of sorrow, owning once more the sin that had caused it; but the throne of God perpetually endures: and now—for it ought to be a question—"hast Thou utterly rejected us? wilt Thou be exceeding wroth against us?"

3. *Ezekiel.*

Ezekiel fills, indisputably, the third place among the prophets. It is all through the application of a text from Leviticus. The prophet is here at the same time a priest, and as a priest he is bidden to examine as to the leprosy of Israel. The proofs, alas! are multiplied, the case is plain: then the glory of God, insulted to His face by the most open idolatry and the most flagrant sins, leaves the city; the leper is put outside the camp.

But in God there is help, though not in man. It is His grace which has made provision for sin, when it has come to extremity and is out before Him: "If the leprosy break out abroad in the skin, and the leprosy cover all the skin of him that hath the plague, from the head even to the feet, wherever the priest looketh; then the priest shall consider, and if the leprosy have covered all his flesh, he shall pronounce him clean that hath the plague." In Ezekiel, this is now fulfilled to Israel. The prophet does not close, as Jeremiah does, with sorrow, but sees the people brought back by the omnipotent grace of God, a new heart given them, and a new spirit put within them; the nation arises as from the dead; Judah and Ephraim are joined together; and now a new temple receives the glory of God, and from it issue the streams of blessing which revivify the sea of death itself.

Thus Ezekiel needs no vindication as the third book of the prophetic series. It is the book of the sanctuary; of the glory of God, of national resurrection; while throughout, Leviticus furnishes its text in the commandments as to leprosy and the cleansing of the leper.

4. *Daniel.*

Daniel completes the series of the greater prophets

with the prophetic history of the times of the Gentiles. He thus fully answers to his numerical place, and to the books of the captivity in the historical series. It is the nations of the earth we have before us; with Israel dispersed among them, though watched over as be-loved for the fathers' sakes, because the gifts and calling of God are without repentance. Daniel, how-ever, only indicates their blessing as to come, never enters into it.

His great theme is the testing of the Gentile powers in the empire now committed to their hands. And here the failure is complete, and represented in every picture. The degeneration of material in the image shown to Nebuchadnezzar; the historical chapters, which portray the moral decline; the wild beasts of Daniel's vision, replacing with their fierce, wild, bestial life the form (but lifeless) of the man in that of the king; these things are features of his book scarcely to be overlooked. The closing chapters furnish specific details especially of the time of the end, to which all hastens; for prophecy only *rests* in the kingdom of God.

5. *The Minor Prophets.*

We come now to the Minor Prophets, whose prophecies we have seen were looked at by the Jews as forming but one book. We are not compelled to take their reasons for it, which are merely trivial, and necessitate another if the arrangement itself is to be justified. Let us see, then, if it be possible to find another.

As *one* book, they must find the fifth place in the prophets: the first four are plainly filled. The fifth place speaks of *governmental ways:* here at least seems a subject various enough for a twelvefold exposition. Then the number 12 itself speaks of government, and that it refers to such manifest government of God as was seen in the past in Israel, and as will be seen again in millennial times, does not conflict with this; for this is at once what most of the prophets start from and all look forward to. At least we may take this, then, as a hint of their true place.

Furthermore, when we consider that even as *minor* prophets their scope is not the large and general one of the greater books, but that they take up and specialize some distinctive parts of God's one great whole of wisdom in the control of earthly events, what more accords with the character thus assigned them?

Let us look, then, at the books themselves.

And here, if they really stand together as a whole, it would seem that we might expect this number 12 to divide as other twelves do—into 4 x 3. Do they indeed divide so?

The question necessitates first another: Is there any difference of order possible? or are we to take them as they stand in our Bibles generally?

As to the last six, there is no difference; as to the first, in the Septuagint, the order is different. Hosea, Amos, Micah, Joel, Obadiah, Jonah, instead of, as with us, Hosea, Joel, Amos, Obadiah, Jonah, Micah.

Is there any account of this order to be given?

The answer is, that as to the whole of the Minor Prophets, there is little satisfactory account, except that in both arrangements the order is so far chronological, that "the prophets of the pre-Assyrian and Assyrian times (Hosea to Nahum) are placed first, as

being earliest; then follow those of the Chaldean
period (Habakkuk and Zephaniah); and lastly, the
series is closed by the three prophets after the captivity (Haggai, Zechariah, and Malachi), arranged in
the order in which they appeared" (*Keil*).

Further than this, the order is not strictly chrono·
logical; which, if carried out, would, moreover, involve,
the mixing together of the greater and lesser books
The reasons given for the actual arrangement other·
wise are merely trivial, while yet that Keil does little
more than copy them from Delitzsch shows clearly that
nothing better, however, is to be found.   Who could
accept such reasons as these from the latter: that
Hosea is placed first, as the largest book in the collec·
tion; Joel follows because of the contrast of the
"dewy, verdant, and flowery imagery with which the
book of Hosea closes" and the "all-parching heat,
and the all-consuming swarms of insects" in Joel?
Amos then follows, as taking up one of the utterances
with which Joel closes; then Obadiah, as an expansion of Amos ix. 12—"That they may possess the
remnant of Edom;" then Jonah, because Obadiah
speaks of a "messenger sent among the nations," and
Jonah was such a messenger!

Plainly, if this is the best account to be given, it is
not a very satisfactory one.   Can we find any thing
better?

Beginning at the end, then, the last three prophets,
as prophets of the *captivity*, seem to give clearly a
fourth section of just the requisite number, while the
second three in the Septuagint order seem all to speak
of the Gentile enemy.   The third three are in both

arrangements the same. Let us take, then, the twelve in this order and division, and see what the numbers say.

(1) The first three will then be Hosea, Amos, and Micah. These are also generally the largest in scope, and, with the exception of Zechariah, the largest actually. This is still encouragement: let us look further, therefore.

Of the three, Hosea is the longest, if not also the widest, in scope. As the first of all, and so far introductory, the close is very significant as to the character of the whole series: "Who is wise, and he shall understand these things? prudent, and he shall know them? *for the ways of the Lord are right*, and the just shall walk in them; but the wicked shall fall therein."

Now it is quite according to the style of Scripture to give us in the introductory portion of any book the main thought of it. It is the goodness of God, who would thus guide His people at the outset into the meaning of what he has to say to them. Look especially at the epistles, and see how plain this is there. And thus to find in Hosea this Deuteronomic strain, and as the purport of his prophecy, cannot but give further satisfaction as to the place of these books.

The name of Hosea means "help, salvation." It was the original name of Israel's leader into the land of Caanan, which by the addition to it of the covenant-name of God became "Jehoshua." We are familiar with another prophet, with a name similar in meaning, and it is instructive to compare in this respect Isaiah, or even Joshua, and Hosea.

"Hosea" is "salvation;" "Isaiah," "*Jehovah's* salvation." I cannot but believe that the difference is indicated in their books. Isaiah is largely—I do not mean wholly—*objective*: it is an *objective* salvation with which he is mainly occupied, and this is what fills his book so with joy and sunshine. The person and work of Christ are dwelt on much. Hosea is the *subjective* side of this salvation, and what he dwells on is repentance and return to God. Independence and wandering of heart are to be judged, and the "valley of Achor the door of hope." Then where it was said unto them, "Ye are not My people," it shall be said unto them, "Ye are the sons of the living God." "For the children of Israel shall abide many days without a king, and without a prince, and without a sacrifice, and without an image, and without an ephod, and without teraphim; afterward shall the children of Israel return and seek the Lord their God and David their king, and shall fear the Lord and His goodness in the latter days."

This is a return to the principle of victory in Joshua, and it has just now struck me that we have had a direct reference to Joshua in the valley of Achor given as their hope. Independence judged and exchanged for true subjection, then the glorious throne to which they turn shall be full of power for them. And this is the first principle, surely, of divine government,— subjection to the throne as the way of blessing.

Amos, in his long exposure of the moral condition of the people, is very like Hosea, and like him addresses the whole of the divided kingdom; but he goes beyond this, and takes up briefly the nations occupying Israel's territory, judges them for their enmity and cruelty.

Then Judah and Israel pass under review, and their sins are detailed. Finally, the tabernacle of David is to be raised up, the land inhabited, and their enemies dispossessed.

Amos is thus very kindred to Hosea, the same in character very much, but less strongly pronounced, and taking into account the enemies as Hosea does not. It thus seems to occupy its numerical place, and vindicate the Septuagint order. It has none of the characters of a *third* book, as I think, which the Hebrew arrangement makes it.

Micah comes in either order as a third book, but of the second section in our common Bibles, in the Septuagint, of the first. It takes in "Samaria and Jerusalem." Characteristically, it begins with "Let the Lord God be witness against you, the Lord from *His holy temple.*" Afterward, for the common corruption of rulers, priests, and prophets, the desolation of the city is shown with special mention of the "mountain of the Lord's house," in the last days to be exalted in the top of the mountains, and people to flow unto it.

The rejection of Christ is also seen, and His divine character; and Israel is given up until her time of travail is over, then the remnant of His brethren (now found only among Christians,) shall be numbered again among the children of Israel. Christ shall be their final "peace," when in the midst of the very evils which their rejection of Him has brought upon them.

All through, the pleading with them because of their sins is maintained much as in Hosea and Amos, but still more tenderly, and Israel's sorrows are seen more fully as the travail-pains out of which the blessing comes : they are more the needed discipline which is to be fruitful. Every where, I may say, there is more the being face to face with God; His character is manifested more. "Micah," "who is like Jehovah?" is surely significant. And Christ Himself is revealed in His proper glory, and as the true key (in His rejection,) of their present condition.

This, then, is the first section of these prophets.

(2) In the second three, the prophecies are much shorter, and less varied; though Joel, the representative of the former section, in the present, partakes most of its character. But in all three, the enemy now fills the scene in a manner very far from being the case in the former books. The purpose of each book is, however, very distinct, and proportionately they answer to their numerical place with equal plainness.

Joel thus speaks, under the type of what was, no doubt, an actual locust-judgment, of the northern enemy of the latter days. Bnt he is but a rod in the hands of God for endless blessing to the people, and in turning to Him, calling on the name of the Lord, they are saved. Then the Lord recompenses their enemies, Egypt is a desolation, and Edom a desolate wilderness, because of their violence against the children of Judah ; and Jehovah dwelling in Zion, no foot of stranger desecrates her any more.

Obadiah now takes up Edom, and we learn that as the inveterate enemy of Israel, Edom is to be utterly destroyed, and the hand of Israel to inflict the judgment. The measure they meet is measured to them again, and by those also against whom has been their enmity.

But *Jonah* has how different a story to recite. It is

his own mainly,—in fact, of the people to whom he belongs. It is through Israel's salvation that blessing will come to the nations of the earth, as the eleventh of Romans plainly says; and thus she will become to them the prophet of repentance. Refusing her original call to this, and fleeing vainly from God, she is cast into the sea of the nations, yet preserved miraculously in the very jaws of destruction, and, when she has learned that "salvation is of the Lord," brought up as by resurrection. Thus she becomes the messenger to them, and the following history touchingly declares how she is brought to be in fellowship with the Lord's mercy in their case.

Thus the second series fittingly ends in the display of mercy both to Israel and the nations, while in this third prophet we have God made known both in the power of resurrection and the tender compassion which is His. The numerical seal is here most legibly impressed.

(3) The third series follows, the same now in both Greek and Hebrew,—Nahum, Habakkuk, and Zephaniah. In these we shall find that it is the character of God which is in question and made known by His judgment.

First, *Nahum* shows us, in the Assyrian, the pride of man which breaks out in enmity to God, and the prophecy opens with a sublime description of the holiness and goodness of God against whom man rebels. But His holiness must be against sin, or it would not be that, and the power of the throne must be maintained against rebellion. Thus the foreseen, foreordained judgment surely comes.

Secondly, *Habakkuk* shows us the character of God maintained against all that seems to be in contradiction to it. And here comes forth the beautiful word which is the text for the apostle afterward, that "the just shall live by *faith*." But how great the difficulties seem! The Assyrian is gone, but the Chaldean follows him, and the wicked devours one more righteous than himself. What then? Yet the woe is on the wicked, and the whole earth shall be filled with the glory of the Lord. Faith's embrace becomes firmer, and the glorious apparition of God in His majesty and power rises before it; the soul breaks forth into a song: "Although the fig-tree blossom not, nor fruit be in the vines; the labor of the olive fail, and the fields yield no food; the flock be cut off from the fold, and no herd be in the stalls; *yet* I will rejoice in Jehovah, I will joy in the God of my salvation."

Then, thirdly, *Zephaniah* shows us the sanctifying result. The day of the Lord is upon all the earth, a day of wrath because of man's sin; and amid the judgment of the nations, can Jerusalem possibly escape? No! and yet divine love will have its way also: "All the earth shall be devoured with the fire of My jealousy;" but—"then I will turn to the peoples a pure language, that they may call upon the name of the Lord to serve Him with one consent. In that day shalt thou not be ashamed for all thy doings wherein thou hast transgressed against Me; for then will I take out of the midst of thee them that rejoice in thy pride, and thou shalt no more be haughty because of My holy mountain. I will also leave in the midst of thee an afflicted and poor people, and they shall trust in the name of the Lord. The remnant of Israel shall not do iniquity, nor speak lies; neither shall a deceitful tongue be found in their mouth: for they shall feed and lie down, and none shall make them afraid."

Then the song again bursts forth, (well it may!) "The King of Israel, even the Lord, is in the midst of thee: thou shalt not see evil any more. . . . . The Lord thy God in the midst of thee is mighty; He will save, He will rejoice over thee with joy; He will rest in His love; He will joy over thee with singing."

Surely, if the strength of faith is exhibited in Habakkuk, the sanctifying power of God's judgments and the full display of His heart are brought out in Zephaniah.

(4) And now there remain, as a fourth section, the prophets of the captivity—Haggai, Zechariah, and Malachi. They answer, as already said, to the three historical books of the same period. Ezra and Haggai speak mainly of the temple; Nehemiah and Zechariah, of the city; while in Esther and Malachi every thing seems once more ruined and gone, and yet God works out (as one may say, in silence,) His unrepenting purposes of blessing.

All make evident the utter failure, even among the returned captives, and the utter silence which follows after Malachi in Israel is the mouth stopped, as it were, even in intercession. But it does not stop without a fresh prediction of the blessing to come, for the gifts and calling of God are without repentance.

Haggai has, as it were, the mark of the new section which it opens in the four messages of which it is made up. The first reproves the people for their leaving the building of the Lord's house to build their own. As soon as they give heed, Jehovah declares that He is with them. The second declares the shaking of the nations, and the coming of the Desire of all, and consequently the latter glory of the house to be greater than all before. The *third* reasons with them that holiness cannot sanctify what is evil; but evil, on the other hand, defiles what is holy. Their previous state had hindered blessing; now, they would find it. While the fourth announces once more the shaking of the heavens and the earth, but the abiding of Christ, (typified by Zerubbabel,) the seal of a new condition.

Zechariah, in the second place, speaks of the salvation and blessing of Jerusalem, God's grace in the putting away of sin being very distinctly stated. Afterward he shows the rejection of Christ and its consequences, and Antichrist's reception. Finally, the repentance of the people when Christ is seen in glory, and their deliverance in the final siege by His appearing for them.

Finally, in the third place, *Malachi* reproves the returned people for their iniquity in their holy things; prophesies incense to Jehovah's name and a pure offering every where, and the coming of the Lord to His temple when the sons of Levi shall be purified and the offering of Judah and Jerusalem be again acceptable. The Lord owns amid the corruption the remnant that fear Him, and assures them that by and by the distinction He makes between the righteous and the wicked shall be manifest; for the day comes that shall consume the wicked, and to those that fear Him the Sun of Righteousness shall arise with healing in His wings.

Elijah the prophet would be sent for spiritual restoration before that great and notable day, that the land might not be smitten with a curse.

Thus the Prophets end, and brief as the account has been, I believe your conviction will be my own, that the numerical seal is upon all, from first to last; more evident, of course, in certain books, and yet not obscurely upon all. One thing that is greatly assuring is, that the more fully a book is known, the more clearly we find the impress of it. We shall find this in the books which follow, therefore, clearer than ever, because the books are clearer. May the Lord guide us by His Spirit as we pursue our study on to the end of His precious and holy Word.

LECTURE VI

The Psalm-Books, Gospels, and Acts

WE are now, beloved brethren, to examine that division of the Old Testament which stands last in all Hebrew Bibles, and last in our Lord's words in the last chapter of Luke, "the law of Moses, the prophets, and the psalms." He does not use indeed the Jewish term for this last division, which was called by the Jews (vaguely enough), "the writings," or "Scriptures,"—*Kethubim;* and we have no certain proof that He meant to speak of more than the actual book of Psalms, in which "the things concerning Himself" are of all of them the fullest and plainest. Still the order coincides with that of the Hebrew, and we have seen good reason already for accepting it. The Psalms, with the four kindred books, are really, in their significance, a fourth division of the Old Testament. If the other books of the *Kethubim* are to be added to these, then indeed the significance is destroyed, but this alone is a better reason for *not* adding them than any we can find for doing so.

As they stand in our Bibles also their numerical meaning is again destroyed, while in the order I have before proposed they form a real Pentateuch, as I desire now to show; a Pentateuch of which the book of Psalms is the Genesis, Job the Exodus, Solomon's Song the Leviticus, Ecclesiastes the Numbers, and Proverbs the Deuteronomy.

It needs not many words to show that these books form a series distinct from every other in the Bible. They are not history, it is plain, even the narrative in the book of Job being quite subservient to the moral problem. Nor are they *in form* prophecy, although the Psalms at least are thoroughly prophetic; but in them the prophecy is not announced as such, but left to come out afterward to the faith that can read it there, just as the types of law and history, which last (as in the person of David) are conspicuous in the Psalms.

Thus, negatively, these books are separated from all other books. As poetical, they are separated also from the historical, but not from the prophetical part of the Old Testament, or at least by no clear line. They are united together by their character as *experience* books, which applies clearly to them all, however different the experience may be in each. It is the individual path through the world that is exhibited in them, though the "Song" can only be said to be this in a certain sense, and the first three books are all higher in character than the last two. The Psalms, however, with the usual Genesis-largeness, furnish parallels to all the rest.

"Trial" is stamped fully on all, and exercise of heart is begotten of this, the number 5 not only giving the number of books in the section, but the number of divisions of the books in general, as in the five books of the Psalms proper, which the Revised Version now brings before the English reader. The dark and difficult problems of which the world is full are here allowed to have utterance by the lips of man himself, and their solution is given *in some sense or other;* not always by the vail being lifted indeed, but always by God being brought into them, and man learning, as in Job and in Ecclesiastes, his true place before Him.

The five books are nevertheless very distinct from one another—necessarily so, I may say, from what they are: for how various are the experiences and exercises through which we pass! This distinctness makes our task proportionately easier. Indeed, it is hardly possible here to mistake what is before us.

1. *Psalms.*

No one that knows the Psalms will doubt that they have all the largeness of the Genesis-books. That they are in fact thus large with the fulness of the divine counsels which they contain is the result of their being prophetic, as they are, more fully than is even now generally seen. The reason is, no doubt, the style in which they are written, which may be well understood from the confessedly Messianic psalms. Take for example the twenty-second psalm. It is not a direct prediction, but the Spirit of God leading the Psalmist, in the expression of personal feelings, to go beyond himself, so as to become, whether consciously or not, the representative of One greater than himself. The psalm is thus left as a divine secret, a mystery to be unraveled by faith. The prophecy is made to conform to the character of these experience books.

But so also in many another psalm, in which not Messiah but a saint of the latter days is put before us in an exactly similar manner; so that the experiences, feelings, and exercises proper to the people of God

then are found in the outpourings of the heart of an
Asaph, a Heman, an Ethan, a son of Korah, or even
of David himself.

The people so taken up is Israel—the ten tribes or
the two,—seen in sorrows which will come upon them
in the great time of Jacob's trouble, out of which he
will be delivered and brought into lasting blessing. It
is a time when, the Church having been removed to
heaven, and the times of the Gentiles fast hastening to
an end, Israel will pass through the trials which will
purify and prepare them for the blessing. It is the
time of unparalleled tribulation of which the twenty-
fourth of Matthew speaks, and the mingled and various
character of it is such, that believers of every time have
been finding in its prophetic anticipation a provision
made for the most diversified conditions, while the
saints of that time will find in it a special provision for
peculiar need. The sufferings and the grace of Christ
are seen in special relation to these, while of course
faith's portion ever, and its joy. But the blessing
flowing out is seen in connection with Israel and the
earth in the constant style of Old-Testament promises.
Our own are better and heavenly ones.

But thus the range of the Psalms is an exceedingly
wide one, and in striking contrast in this respect with
the other books of its division. More even than with
Isaiah is their theme salvation, though even here, in
the Christian sense, we must not expect to find it in its
fulness. The blessedness of one whose iniquity is
forgiven and whose sin is covered we do find, and,
with the justification of Abraham and Habakkuk's
word of the just who live by faith. it is part of the

threefold text from the Old Testament on which Paul
preaches in the epistle to the Romans.   All lines of
Old-Testament truth meet us in the Psalms, and what
has been said of Israel's great prophet is just as true
of her great Psalmist also.

But what makes them *psalms* gives them surely their
character.   They are heart-melodies addressed to God;
so that in the saddest of them, still God reigns: amid
all fears and questionings and darkness and difficulty,
it is to Him ever that the soul turns; and thus there
comes into its wildest outpourings a rhythm and tender
sweetness which awakes nature around, as in the utterance of harp or other instrument, into responsive
accompaniment.   Thus the Psalms proclaim God
sovereign, and the book of Psalms as such comes first
among the experience books.   With assurance of victory in all the strife of which these books are full, the
singers are put in the forefront of the oattle.

I have already mentioned how the book of Psalms
was used of God in leading me into this structure of
Scripture, and that it was in the five books into which
it is divided that I first found the Pentateuchal mould
in which we now see, as I trust, so large a part of it is
cast.   I feel now in some sense bound to show you in
how beautiful and complete a way the " Pentateuch of
David" answers to its name.

" Among the fathers," says Delitzsch, " Gregory of
Nyssa has attempted to show that the Psalter, in its
five books, leads upward, as by five steps, to moral
perfection; and down to the most recent times, attempts have been made to trace in the five books a
gradation of principal thoughts, which run through the

whole collection. We fear that in this direction investigation has set before itself an unattainable end."

All do not, however, acquiesce in this. Another can say, on the other hand, "The distinction of subject I found in them had led me to divide the whole book of Psalms in the same way [into five books] before my attention had been drawn to the well-known fact of its being so divided in the Hebrew Bible. But this principle of order is carried out also in the details of each of the books."*

Of this we may be assured; and the writer in question has furnished us largely with the means of following out this order. I propose, however, to give you my own thoughts as to the books in my own fashion, in order to show you the numerical stamp and the connection with the books of Moses, both of which throw much light upon them.

The first book embraces the first forty-one psalms; the second, the thirty-one following; the third, seventeen more; the fourth, similarly, seventeen; the fifth, the remainder—forty-four in number.

The first book divides again into three, which are easily distinguished from one another, the third division being much larger than the first two together.

They are distinguished thus :—

The first eight psalms give us as an introduction Christ rejected by the nations, exalted of God, but waiting to take the kingdom which is His,—waiting in a long-suffering which is salvation. This is the second psalm; in the eighth, we see Him as the Son of man

---

* "A Synopsis of the Books of the Bible." By J. N. Darby. Vol. ii. p. 59.

set in power over all the works of God's hands. This is "the world to come" of Heb. ii.,—the millennial kingdom.

Between these two come *five* psalms which give the exercises of saints in the meantime between Christ's suffering and glory. These, then, are the subjects of the introductory series.

The second division is from psalm ix. to xv.; ix. and x. giving us the circumstances of the latter days in Israel, and the enemy's power; another five psalms following, giving us their exercise in view of this. Observe how the 5 is repeated here.

The third division carries us to the close of the book; and here we have (as in neither of the others,) Christ *in the midst of the people*, and His suffering in grace which is the secret of all their blessings. And this divides again into three parts : first, a Messianic series of *nine*, and this really 3 x 3 ; secondly, the experience psalms proper, which are now in this third division *three* times 5 ; and then two closing psalms (xl. and xli.) which are again Messianic.

I wish I could pause, to show you a little the details; but we may easily see that in the book as a whole we have the *counsels* of God, which are fulfilled in Christ, the basis of blessing for His people (Israel).

The second book (Ps. xlii.–lxxii.) carries us on fully to the last days, and shows us their deliverance by Christ when in the sorrows of their final trial, the fruit of their sins. I cannot go into the details, but it is quite characteristically the Exodus-book, and the psalms of the sons of Korah (spared in the wilderness when their father sinned,) which open the book are very suitably the expression of this grace.

The theme of the third book (Ps. lxxiii.–lxxxix.) is the *holiness* of God, which is fully shown in all His dealings with the people in the eleven psalms of Asaph which form the first division; while the last six psalms show how Christ as the Servant of God has maintained this holiness even to suffering under the broken law (lxxxviii.). This is the Leviticus of the Psalms.

The fourth, as the Numbers-book (Ps. xc.–cvi.), is a most exquisite illustration of the breadth and variety with which Scripture can treat one common subject. The book is similarly divided to the last into two portions of eleven and six psalms respectively. The first is the creation-, the second the redemption-part; but redemption now takes effect upon creation itself, and the wilderness is at an end forever.

The book opens with the ninetieth psalm, a genuine psalm of the wilderness. It is the lament over the generation dying out there under the wrath of God; but it is but the expression of the common doom. God who made man out of the dust is turning him back to it again. Yet is He surely man's dwelling-place in all generations! How strange a disorder has sin introduced!

The ninety-first psalm then takes up the theme, "He who dwelleth in the secret place of the Most High shall abide under the shadow of the Almighty." But who knows this secret place, so as to obtain this sure protection? Man as a race has lost the very knowledge of God's name. "When I come unto the children of Israel," says Moses, "and shall say unto them, The God of your fathers hath sent me unto you, and they shall say to me, What is His name? what shall I say unto them?" God has lost His name for men, but His name is just the expression of what He is. This, then, is the secret of man's ruin; he is departed far from God, and has become a stranger to Him.

But in the ninety-first psalm another voice is heard. The unbelief of Israel accounted for Christ's miracles by saying that He had stolen the name of God. In fact it was true He had it, but as His natural portion which He had never lost. " I say of Jehovah "—not " I *will* say"—" He is my refuge and strength, my God, in Him do I trust." Here is the Second Man who has never fallen. Therefore all the power of God is on His side: " Because He has set His love upon Me, therefore will I deliver Him; I will set Him on high, because He hath *known My name.*"

The ninety-second—a Sabbath psalm—carries this further: the Second Man, as a new head of blessing, secures the blessing and purification of the earth. The wicked are to be destroyed out of it, the righteous to flourish. And in the ninety-third, Jehovah reigns there, and the world is established that it cannot be moved.

The following psalms—seven in number—then give the coming of Jehovah to the earth, and how all things break into song before Him.

But the second division has a deeper secret yet to tell: *Jehovah and this Second Man are one!* And how beautifully is this shown!

First, the hundred and first psalm shows the Second Man in His qualifications for rule upon the earth; in the hundred and second, the time has come, Zion is to be built up again, the nations gathered together to serve the Lord. But where is He that is to rule? Is it a Man cast down in the divine wrath, His strength weakened in the way, His days shortened? Hear Him as He pleads, "O My God, take Me not away in the midst of My days! Thy years are throughout all generations."

But what says the answer of God to Him? It is here that the amazing secret is discovered. This humbled Man is owned in His humiliation as Jehovah's Fellow. "Of old hast Thou laid the foundations of the earth, and the heavens are the work of Thy hands: they shall perish, but Thou endurest!"

How wonderful is this! and how great are its consequences! Creator and Redeemer are one: the hands that receive the government of the earth are almighty ones: there is an indefectible Head of blessing: God and man are brought how unutterably near! Thus the hundred and third psalm begins now its tale of grace and blessing; the hundred and fourth celebrates Jehovah—the Redeemer—as the Creator; the hundred and fifth is His appeal to Israel, and the final psalm their confession and repentance.

And now the fifth book begins—Israel just ready to take possession of the land after their long dispersion —the Deuteronomic rehearsal of the Lord's ways with men. I need only say that not merely the opening psalm, but the whole book has this character. Only it ends now with full blessing—the blessings of the new covenant—and with the full halleluiah-chorus from all the earth.

2. *Job.*

That the book of Job gives the same story of trial and

exercise, no one will question; nor that, as a second book, it fills its place in bringing before us as it does the work and power of the enemy. In none is this more openly seen, as we are all aware. A comparison with Ecclesiastes, the fourth book of the series, develops some points of special interest, which help to make clear the character of each.

Job is the *best* man on earth, pronounced so of God Himself; Solomon is the wisest, and declared so in the Word of God. In Job his goodness is tested, as in Ecclesiastes is Solomon's wisdom; and, like all things human, each breaks down under the test.

Now these correspond to the two forms of trial specially insisted on in the New Testament as a preparation for Christ. In Rom. v., you have the first in its result: "When we were yet without strength, in due time Christ died for the ungodly." In 1 Cor. i., you have the second in its result: "When in the wisdom of God the world by wisdom knew not God, it pleased God by the foolishness of the preaching to save them that believe." Thus men are proved as to moral character, and as to the value of that for which they sacrificed innocence. And here in Job, the best man on earth is vile, and repents in dust and ashes; in Ecclesiastes, the wisest man can only see vanity written on all under the sun.

This, then, is the main feature of the book of Job: that the best man on earth can on that ground claim no exemption from the severest trials; and that if he assume it, he has yet only to see God aright, and he will abhor himself and repent in dust and ashes. To this clearing of the eyes, God makes frequent use of trial, although it be but the plow before the sowing, not itself the sowing.

In the line of gospel-truth all this is. The gospel itself we may find dimly in Elihu's words, and parabolically in God's ways with Job when brought thus to repentance.

3. *Solomon's Song.*

In Solomon's Song all true intelligence has seen the picture of occupation with the Beloved. And thus it is a song—yea, the Song of songs; such an one as in the sanctuary alone one sings: for the presence of God is the true home of liberty and joy. In Job, we find the introduction to it indeed in sorrow, but that is another thing. Here also exercise of heart is not over, for it is not the full Christian place that is recognized here, but—as the same writer referred to a short time since says,—" the re-establishment of the relations between Christ and the remnant [of Israel], in order that by exercise of heart—necessary on account of their position—they may be confirmed in the assurance of His love, and in the knowledge that all is of grace, a grace that can never fail. Then is He fully known as Solomon. His heart becomes like the chariot of His willing people (Ammi-nadib) which carries Him away."

Occupation with the Lord is the token of the sanctuary, and we shall find it one of the commonest marks of a third section. This is clearly the place of the book, therefore, in this division.

4. *Ecclesiastes.*

Ecclesiastes is even more plainly the fourth book. In it not only, as we have seen, is man's wisdom proved at fault, but the world itself is tried, and " vanity " is found written upon all. "Vanity of vanities: *all* is vanity." The trial is made by one with all the resources of a kingdom such as Solomon's. The men of the world require plenty of material to furnish out the happiness they seek; but in this respect, "what can the man do that cometh after the king?" He has wisdom also to make use of these resources, and a heart set upon doing it. If the result is after all failure, who then shall succeed?

Death is upon every thing; and the more precious any thing is, the more terrible to know that it must pass away. Whether lost wholly and at once, or filched away little by little by the flying moments, still all that we prize is doomed; and *we* are doomed. To every thing there is a time, and for every thing the time goes by. And God has fixed the place and time of all in this cycle of things that pass and return, among the generations which yet do not return. Eternity, too, is set in man's heart, compassed as he is by that which is for the moment; but eternity no wisdom of his can pierce: it is the wisdom of which death is the price paid, and it cannot elude or look beyond it. Death brings down all to its level—wise and fool, and man and beast: what difference? save that the beast can fill his place for a time with no regrets and no anticipations, and man cannot. Death he hates and dreads, and conscience forebodes judgment.

It is true, thank God! that Ecclesiastes does not leave things here. God has spoken, and faith has keener sight than any wisdom of man. Still the world as such is gone, therefore, for faith also. To do God's will in it, "this is the whole of man."

5. *Proverbs.*

And now Proverbs closes with lessons as to this will of God, the maxims of a wisdom higher than human, yet proved also in experience, and which declare the path for him who seeks it. Yet how plainly do we see in this book of moral results, the Deuteronomy, in a sense, of the whole Old Testament, that, except in type and shadow, the heavenly things are not yet come. The glory shines not yet on a road tracked by pilgrim feet. Prophecy and promise do but beckon onward ; and the Old Covenant testifies, in its brightest revelations, to what is beyond itself.

The New Testament.

We come, then, to the New Testament. We have traced the numerical structure all the way through the Old, with whatever imperfection in the way of doing it. We have even begun already to see that the same stamp is on the New ; the full light being here come, we ought to see it very plainly.

In the Old Testament we have found four Penta-teuchs ; in the New, spite of its twenty-seven books, there is but one ; and this though also a true *fifth*, is, because of the twofold primary division of Scripture, a single isolated one. And this, it would seem, must be as significant as the Old-Testament four. I do not doubt it to be so, and would venture a thought on the significance of the number 1 in this connection.

The New Testament has its distinctive character in this, that it is the Gospel of grace, which as such manifests God to men. We have already seen this also, and how well it suits a *second* division of Scripture and

with its twenty-seven books.   But what, then, is to be
the moral effect of such a revelation?   Surely this,
that God so revealed be *enthroned* supreme in the
hearts of those who receive this testimony, in such a
way as could never have been before.   Significantly,
the ark and mercy-seat, which represent Christ, as we
are all agreed, were in Israel the throne of God.   He
sat between the cherubim.   And is it not in Christ that
God reigns, as otherwise He has never reigned? both
as glorified in His obedience, and in that dear name of
"Father" in which we have at once the revelation of
God and His relation to us?   And what title would
like this convey the new obedience to which we are
called?—the *entire* obedience due from children; the
endeared obedience which is not only freedom, but
freedom as the joy of love?

Thus we find that whereas under the law there were
things permitted of which it could be said, "Moses
for the hardness of your heart gave you this precept,"
now nothing is to be conceded to the hardness of men's
hearts.   "That which is born of the flesh is" indeed
still "flesh;" but there is a new birth of the Spirit, and
a new power of God for men; and it is to be shown in
this, that in the new child's place known, and with the
Spirit of sonship, God is to be now wholly God.   "Ye
have heard that it hath been said to them of old time
. . . . ; but I say unto you."   "Be ye therefore perfect, even as your Father in heaven is perfect."

This, then, is what I believe the *one* Pentateuch of
the New Testament suggests to us, spreading out as it
does in its glorious compass of twenty-seven books,
like the various fruits of the tree of life which the

river of life sustains and fructifies. Of this Pentateuch,—

The Gospels

are of course the Genesis. The Lord's life on earth is
what John speaks of afterward in his epistle as "the
beginning;" and with this, although the manifestation
of what is not temporal but eternal, the centuries re-
new themselves. The first man has been told out, and
his history is really over: the Second Man is come,
and replaces him. With this, the inarticulate voices of
the past find utterance; the vail is removed, the darkness passed; the substance replaces the shadows; the
Word made flesh tabernacles among us, and we behold
His glory, the glory as of the Only Begotten with the
Father, full of grace and truth.

The Gospels are *four*, because He in whom this
glory shines is come to put Himself into the hands of
His creatures,—to be seen, gazed on, handled by their
hands; to submit Himself to every species of trial,—in
order that in all this His glory may be fully recognized.
Thus each of these Gospels has its different story to
tell, both of Person and work,—its different aspect to
give to the beholder,—that we may be able more to
take in and appreciate as He would have us the Christ
of God.

1. The Synoptic Gospels.

But these four Gospels are, as already has been noted,
not 2 and 2, which would be true division, and the Son
of God cannot be in fact divided. But they are a 3
and 1, the divine numbers being brought out thus: how
truly the effect of these part-representations to bring

out the divine glory of the Man, Christ Jesus, every believing heart bears witness.   The Synoptic Gospels, as they are called, stand thus as the first part here: Matthew with its testimony to the King, Mark to the Ministering Servant, Luke to the Man; clearly united among themselves, and proportionately distinct from John's testimony to the Word made flesh.   Yet these *three*, as their number intimates, also declare, each after its own manner, God in Christ.   It surely must be so, or there would be discord, not united witness.

The three agree also in this, and contrast with John, that in them all, as in the parable of the vineyard, which they all give, Christ is seen as God's last testimony to Israel,—His Son, sent after the rejection of all previous messengers, as His last resource.   " Having yet, therefore, one son, his well-beloved, he sent him also last unto them, saying, ' They will reverence my son.' "   Accordingly the whole character of the books is affected by this.   Testing in this way is still going on.   The demonstration of the mind of the flesh as enmity against God is not complete in them until the cross.   Israel is not yet set aside; man is not seen as *dead* in sins ; the decidedly Christian truths of new birth and eternal life are not brought out.   These, with kindred doctrines, characterize John, whose gospel is therefore in the full sense the Christian one,— the full New-Testament second part.   In every way, therefore, the numerical seal is on these books.   Of these, the order almost universally recognized is what we find in our common Bibles—Matthew, Mark, Luke, and John.   We shall find this order in full accordance with the numerals represented.

Matthew.

There is one expression found repeatedly in Matthew's gospel, and although it has its roots in the book of Daniel, never actually found elsewhere. It must surely then be characteristic. This expression is, "The kingdom of heaven."

Matthew may be fairly entitled, "The gospel of the kingdom of heaven." There are three things which are borne witness to in the first chapter as to the King, which are of special importance as defining its character. First, Christ is the Son of David; and the Jews necessarily occupy a foremost position in the book. But secondly, He is also "Son of Abraham," which brings in the blessing of the nations also. Thirdly, because it is heaven's kingdom, its King is also, and above all, Son of God.

Matthew gives us, therefore, the Jewish question prominently, the passing of the kingdom to the Gentiles when the Jews reject; yet also their reception of it in a yet future day. It is the *dispensational* gospel; and this is as much as to say, that of the divine *counsels*, which these dispensations indicate. Matthew is thus the only gospel which gives specifically the Church, which even John does not.

Its governmental aspect is plain throughout. God is on the throne; but though the Father's name is declared, there is not the intimacy yet which this implies. The work of salvation is intimated but as to *be*, not as yet accomplished. Discipleship and obedience are prominent themes; forgiveness of sins is conditional, and may be revoked; and the outflow of God's heart does not yet, as it will do, awaken man's heart in response. In the cross, as I desire more fully presently to show, we have the *trespass*- (that is, the *governmental*) offering.

This may suffice just now, as it is only the place of the book which I am indicating. In looking at those which follow, we shall, however, have occasion briefly to return to this.

Mark.

Mark has been often looked at as if it were little more than an abridgment of Matthew. It is indeed in many respects similar, and yet in some respects also it is as different as can be. Scripture does not admit of mere repetitions or abridgments ; and here will be found a divine purpose and meaning quite distinct and even in contrast with the former gospel.

Thus the dispensational character is not at all in Mark, and the Lord appears only exceptionally as King of Israel, the title itself being simply as con- demnation written upon His cross. Even as Lord He is seldom addressed, and never by His disciples. But He is the Son of God in service, in unequaled volun- tary humiliation, which is His brightest glory, a poverty by which He enriches others. It is on this account that the genealogy which comes first in Matthew is not found at all in Mark. *Love needs no title to serve but the power to do so.* His birth is not given, nor are His earlier years, but the gospel addresses itself at once to His ministry, of which all the tenderness and grace are minutely pictured.

Service in humiliation is thus the theme of Mark, and this fully indicates its place as the second gospel ; but this service finds its lowest place and its deepest meaning in the cross, which just here answers to that aspect of it which the sin-offering presents, as Matthew answers to the trespass-offering.

In the beginning of Leviticus, apart from the meat- (or meal-) offering, which does not speak of death—is not a *sacrifice*, therefore, at all,—four offerings speak of Christ's atoning work. Of these, two are sweet savor-offerings ; the others, not ; because in them the sin and wrong for which they are offered are before the soul, rather than the acceptability of the obedience by which they are met and put away. Now in this way the cross in Matthew and Mark differs from the other gospels, that in them alone we have the cry, " My God, My God, why hast Thou forsaken Me ?" whereas in Luke and John the consciousness of nearness to the Father is found throughout.

But which of these—Matthew or Mark—is the sin,- and which the trespass-offering? and what is the difference between the two ?

It is this, that the *sin*-offering speaks of what is against the *nature* of God, the *trespass*-offering of what is against His *government*.

The trespass-offering speaks of sin as *injury* for which restitution must be made; the sin-offering, of that which God, because of His holiness, cannot look upon, but must put away from Him. Thus only in the sin-offering in Leviticus is the victim burned in the outside place, upon the ground without the sanctifying altar.

But in Matthew and Mark *both* we have the outside place which the Lord takes : why is this?

Because in fact restitution to the throne of God must bear witness to what He is in *nature*. But then this introduces this perplexity: which gospel, then, represents the sin-offering, and which the trespass-offering, if a main feature of the sin-offering be found in both of them?

Now it is evident that Matthew's is the governmental gospel, and this in itself would surely lead us right. Mark's, as the gospel of service, naturally leads to the thought of that which is in its result salvation.

Now it will be found that Mark concentrates our attention upon what sin as sin necessitates before God. Matthew, by its very largeness even, cannot do this. Thus Mark gives us the rent vail, the answer to the darkness of the outside place into which Christ had gone and dispelled it for us; but he does not give, as Matthew, the resurrection of the saints, which is the answer to His *death*. Death is not the full final penalty, but the stamp of divine government upon a fallen creature. Again, in Mark there is no buying of Aceldama—a significant act which was itself a prophecy of what the nation had purchased with the death of Christ —no "His blood be on us and on our children," no judgment even of the traitor. While in Mark also the gospel goes out to every creature.

Notice also, before we close, the order of the offerings in Leviticus and in the gospels here. I have before remarked upon the affinity between 1 and 5 (which is a 4 *plus* 1,) and between 2 and 4, which is a 2 *plus* 2. Now in Leviticus, where the order of the offerings is reversed from that in the gospels, and where the meat-offering must be reckoned in, making thus five in all,

—the trespass-offering stands fifth in order, as it does first here; while the sin-offering stands forth in Leviticus, second here. The peace-offering, which Luke gives us, comes third in both.

Luke.

And Luke's is a third gospel fittingly, although it is not the Word made flesh—God manifest in this sense. It is God manifest inasmuch as the way is opened now to Him, and man is purged and reconciled as the peace-offering exhibits him. The theme of Luke thus unites in the fullest way with that aspect of Christ's person which this gospel specializes,—the truth of His full manhood. This is shown to be what Luke speaks of in the genealogy which—removed indeed from the foremost place it has in Matthew, and *read backward*, because it is not title derived from man, but blessing flowing back to men—links the Lord, not with David merely, nor even with Abraham, but with Adam himself.

Thus you have also the detail of his birth,—His childhood,—His prayers, the full witness of true and pure humanity. And what familiar intimacy with us does all this show! Beside God and the offerer, who each has his part in the peace-offering, the priest who brings both together has his portion also. And the Priest-Mediator is the " *Man*, Christ Jesus." So all the way through, the heart is full and the lips overflow with this deep blessedness. Joy and praise break out with the sense of assured blessing, and the joy is the echo of God's own, as that central story of the prodigal declares it. But this is not alone; in parable and historical fact the heart of God is manifested, and no-where more so than at the cross itself, where a poor thief, enfranchised by His word, follows his Saviour-Lord to paradise.

This closes the Synoptic Gospels. John yet remains with a story still to tell, spite of all that has been told, and a story which, spite of its having been told so long, abides to-day in the same freshness and power as at first.

2. *John.*

But why is John's number not 3, instead of 2, if its subject be God manifest in the flesh? Does not this seem as if it should be the stamp of John rather than of Luke? and in not being so, does it not leave after all some vagueness in the use of these numbers which creates again some doubt and perplexity in the mind?

Now, assuredly, if the numerical system be of God, we must expect it to control our thoughts, not be controlled by them. If it were to be the latter, how little indeed would be the service it could render to us!

And yet it should, for its purpose, also be able to bring conviction of its truth to our minds, as light which manifests,—the self-evidence which is that of all Scripture. Let us see, then, if we can discover a reason for 2, and not 3, being the number of the gospel of John.

Three is indeed the number of divine manifestation, as it is of the Spirit of God, of whose coming also the last part of this gospel is specially full, as we are all aware. And yet *as* the number of the Spirit, it is surely not so suitable as that which speaks of the second Person of the Godhead, the Son of God, just (mark also) as John speaks of Him, the *divine* Son, the Only Begotten, not the First-Begotten. This at once ought to clear away all difficulty and make the numerical meaning plain. The *Word*, again, is John's peculiar title; and if 2 speaks also of humiliation, or a lowly place, then "the Word made flesh" doubly bears the numerical seal upon it. God manifest in Christ is the truth of all the gospels, but the Word made flesh, the only begotten Son incarnate, is, without possibility of contradiction, the exact and characteristic truth of John. How beautifully, then, the divine order approves itself here!

Then we have seen that as a second part the gospel of John is the pre-eminently New-Testament part of the gospels also. Here, Judaism and the law are only contrasted with the "grace and truth" which "came by Jesus Christ." "What is written in your law?" He says to them, and the Jewish feasts and language are all interpreted to us as to Gentiles.

But as in contrast again with the *three* synoptics, John stands alone as by itself the second part. Thus the number 1 is also subordinately stamped upon the book. And so it is assuredly: God's sovereignty is every-where insisted on, that sovereignty in grace whereby He acts in new birth, giving eternal life, another characteristic feature of the gospel. The spiritual Creator is here all through, and the new Genesis outshines the old one.

One thing more only as to John. The cross is here seen in its burnt-offering aspect—that which stands first in the book of Leviticus, and does so because it is the great pattern of perfect obedience, the type of Him in whose heart the will of God was without competitor enthroned. In this way it unites with what we have been just now considering to give the gospel its double numerical stamp of 2 and 1, for obedience is here that "obedience unto death" in which our salvation was accomplished. Here, then, we must close as to the gospels.

The Acts.

The *Acts* is the second division of the New Testament, and it is the only book in its division. Thus its numbers are similar to those of John, except that John belongs first of all to the Genesis-division, while the Acts constitutes in itself the Exodus. It is not Christ whose history is before us, but His people ; and here the character of the book it is impossible to mistake. It is the redemption of believers from under the law, of which the epistle to the Galatians speaks doctrinally. In the Acts, it is the history of that deliverance, the larger part of it being taken up with the instrument God raised up for effecting it. Beginning with Jerusalem and its rejection of the gospel, it shows us then the reception of the Samaritans, afterward the Gentiles openly admitted in Cornelius ; then the raising up of Saul of Tarsus, the scattering of the Jerusalem saints by persecution, the new Gentile assembly formed at Antioch, and the going forth from thence of Saul and Barnabas upon their mission to the nations.

The question then is raised, Is the law to put its yoke upon these new converts ? and that is settled in the negative at Jerusalem itself. The second missionary journey of the apostle follows, the Gentile work enlarges continually ; the Jewish disciples remain zealous of the law, and from the hostility of the unbelievers in Jerusalem the apostle of the Gentiles is saved only by a Roman prison. The last chapter of the Acts narrates the final interview with the Jews at Rome, closing with the apostle's word, " Be it known therefore unto you, that the salvation of God is sent unto the Gentiles, and that they will hear it."

The number 1 is indicated in the Acts by that sovereignty of God every-where seen in it, which has caused some to say that it should be called rather " The Acts of the *Holy Ghost*" than "The Acts of the *Apostles*." I need not enlarge upon this, for all must have remarked it who have seriously and carefully read the book.

LECTURE VII

The Epistles and the Revelation

WE have before us, to-night, beloved brethren, the concluding portion of God's blessed Word; and I cannot but feel, as we enter upon it, how more than inadequate the accouut has been of the previous parts, while it is vain to promise one's self better either as to what remains. Still what account could be given that would not be inadequate? And if a partial representation be in some sort a misrepresentation, it will be sufficient to warn you not to suppose that what has been given is intended for more than a stepping-stone to future progress, and to exhibit the places of the books in that numerical order which I believe the whole Scripture to have. This, spite of all defects, I trust has been so far done, and to be able to carry it through to the end. And the importance of it I think has been shown also. The profit will be found by those who will use in practice what they may have obtained. To wrap it in a napkin will bring no gain.

The order of the epistles varies somewhat in different MSS., as has already been remarked; and in the east, as it would seem, the "catholic" epistles stood before those of Paul. But in the west, the order obtained substantially as it is found in our common Bibles. The order of the Pauline epistles among themselves has been also generally maintained as we have it to-day, although not without minor differences.

No account can be given of any reason for one arrangement rather than another, and no claim of any
divine authority for any arrangement has been made,
so far as I am aware. We do not seem, therefore, in
any way limited as to this.

Now if the numerical system has any value, the
Pauline epistles, and not the catholic, have rightful
claim to be the third division of the New Testament.
The catholic epistles all have for their subject, in some
sense, the path through the world. They stand, in this
way, as a fourth division, plainly. While Paul it is
who establishes the soul before God, opening the
holiest and bringing us in there, as he says himself,
"warning every man, and teaching every man in all
wisdom, that we may present every man perfect in
Christ Jesus." Another has pointed out that the very
doctrine of justification by faith itself is only explicitly
announced by Paul. On the other hand, the walk
through the world is not really the subject of one of
his epistles.

It is Leviticus that gives the different features of the
Lord's great offering as the measure of our acceptance
and of our sanctification to God, and it is Paul who
interprets this into the plain speech of the New Testament. His epistles, then, are plainly the third division ;
and is it without design that there are just fourteen of
them (if Hebrews be counted in) ? that is *twice seven*,
which according to the significance of the numbers
would mean, " *The testimony of a divine work accomplished.*" Their character could hardly be more
concisely given.

But it must not be supposed that they divide into

two sevens: they actually divide into two Pentateuchs, the books of Moses once more being the mould into which these New-Testament books are cast. The three double books rank here as one section each, and one other small book, Philemon, takes its place as a supplement to a larger one—Colossians.

First come the *individual* epistles, by which I do not mean those written to individuals however; in fact, only one of them is so; but those which speak of individual place and its results. They may, indeed, be classed better perhaps as *positional* epistles, if only, as I have said, the practical consequences are reckoned in with this.

The second class are those that speak of *collective* truths, or those that exhibit the Christian as one of a company or fellowship—the family of God, the house of God, the body of Christ.

In the first rank I would put—

    1. Romans.
    2. Galatians.
    3. Ephesians.
    4. Colossians, with—
        [2]Philemon, as a supplement.
    5. Philippians.

In the second rank,—

    1. Thessalonians.
    2. Corinthians.
    3. Hebrews.
    4. Timothy.
    5. Titus.

Let us look briefly now at the separate epistles; and,—

1. *Romans.*

The epistle to the Romans has clearly its natural place at the beginning of all the epistles, its doctrine being the first and fundamental one of acceptance with God. But it has also, and in a beautiful manner, the characteristics of its numerical place.

Counsel and election mark it,—those signs of an omnipotent, omniscient, sovereign God. The doctrine of the eighth and ninth chapters maintains the *will* of God in a way which to some is offensive and to many difficult. Do we not forget that love and holy wisdom must needs characterize *His* will, in whatever way it acts, and it can never be merely arbitrary?

"God's gifts and calling" are thus declared to be "without repentance;" and this is applied to the case of Israel, still "beloved for the fathers' sakes," and their conversion at another day.

But the distinct peculiarity of Romans is not in this, but in the two main points of its teaching, which are plainly *justification* and *the place in Christ.* Neither of these, however, is in itself distinctive. It is in the way they are announced that we shall find what is really so.

As to the first, there is a term used almost confined to this epistle—"the righteousness of God." It is necessary to understand this term, in order to see how it bears upon its numerical place. And indeed the expression itself is perfectly simple. Take the third and fourth verses of the third chapter in illustration: "As it is written, 'That Thou mightest be *justified* in Thy sayings, and mightest overcome when Thou art judged.' But if our unrighteousness commend the *righteousness of God*, what shall we say?" Here, when God is justified in His sayings, His righteousness is commended, and the righteousness of God is just His *righteous character*.

Let this meaning be adhered to every where, and every passage will be simple, and the doctrine plain and uniform throughout. " The righteousness of God " is not, therefore, what is conferred on or imputed to man, but is the character of God Himself. Now when the apostle says, "I am not ashamed of the gospel of Christ, for it is the power of God unto salvation to every one that believeth," he gives as the reason, "for therein is the *righteousness of God revealed*, by faith, to faith." The revelation of the righteousness of God gives thus its peculiar power to the gospel: God's *righteousness* in good news to sinners.

Righteousness ! and why not rather mercy or love ? Certainly these are shown no less ; but there is a most important reason why it should be *righteousness* that is insisted on in the gospel. Did you ever find any one, whatever his sins, afraid of the *mercy* of God? No, you will answer, that is impossible. Or of His *love?* That is equally impossible. Of what, then, is the sinner afraid in God? Plainly, of His *wrath*, and that as against sin is *righteousness*.

Now it is the glory of the gospel, and that in which its power really lies, that in it God's righteousness takes the side of the sinner who will take his place as such before Him. Where is this righteousness declared? The third chapter states this: it is Christ "whom God hath set forth a propitiation, through faith, by His blood "—so the Revised Version rightly renders it,—" to show His righteousness because of the passing over of the sins done aforetime, in the forbearance of God ; for the showing of His righteousness at this present season, that He might Himself be just, and the justifier of him that hath faith in Jesus."

In the blood of Christ, then, God's righteousness is shown. Against sinners? No, surely, but *for* them, because for them that precious blood was shed. And note, that in justification *righteousness* is alone in question. Love can do nothing. Mercy even can do nothing. A sentence of justification can be pronounced by the lips of righteousness *alone*. No wonder, then, that it is this that the apostle insists on as the power of the gospel. It is one thing to say, " I hope in His mercy ;" it is quite another to say, " I rest in His righteousness." And this every poor sinner, taking his place as such before God, is through the blood of Christ entitled to do.

This is the distinctive doctrine of Romans, and this it is which so beautifully marks it as a first epistle. If the number 1, as we have seen, speaks of God's accordance with Himself,—of His oneness in the consistency of all His attributes,—then this is just what the epistle to the Romans shows,—His righteousness actually pronouncing as to believing sinners the sentence of justification, in which His love delights.

But there is a second part of the doctrine of Romans which equally illustrates its numerical place ; and this speaks of our place in Christ before God. Here the doctrine is, that Christ is the new Head of blessing, as Adam was the old head of condemnation.

Life for us in Him is life with all the value of His work attaching to it: "In that He died, He died unto sin once; and in that He liveth, He liveth unto God: even so reckon ye yourselves to be dead indeed unto sin, but alive unto God in Christ Jesus." (Chap. vi. 10, 11, R. V.)

These are the two parts of the doctrine of Romans in its first eight chapters, developed, of course, there, in a way I cannot at this time trace. Of the ninth and beyond I have already briefly spoken. We have here the characteristic features of the book, and I need not press further their correspondence with the place it has at the beginning of the epistles.

2. *Galatians.*

The epistle to the Galatians fills the second place as dwelling upon the contrast between law and grace, the first nevertheless bearing witness to the last, to which it is the ministering handmaid—the Hagar to another Sarah. If the Acts be the historical Exodus from the yoke of bondage, Galatians is its doctrinal statement and justification. This is evident.

The characteristic word in Galatians is the "*cross.*" Other epistles do indeed speak of it: 1 Corinthians, Philippians, and Colossians twice; Éphesians and He-brews once. But in Galatians it has a peculiar place. Testimony as it is to the world's enmity to Christ, it is testimony no less to the opposition of the law to man's salvation. The curse of the law has to be borne by Him who would in His love redeem us from it. "Cursed is every one that hangeth upon a tree." How strange, too, the testimony in the curse, which might seem as if it were suspended through the ages just to fall upon the head of Christ! *Why* should a man be specially cursed who hangs upon a tree? What answer can be given except that thus must be marked that death which was to be borne for sinners, as not simply man's infliction, but God's penalty? What, then, must be the moral result, but that "they that are Christ's *have* crucified the flesh with the affections and lusts?" And as to the world, the apostle expresses it in most vehement words, "God forbid that I should glory, save in the cross of our Lord Jesus Christ, by which the world is crucified to me and I unto the world!" And "Christ gave Himself for our sins, that He might deliver us out of this present evil world, according to the will of our God and Father."

Thus the exodus from the law is an exodus from the world also, and deliverance is thus far complete.

3. *Ephesians.*

And now Ephesians comes in to give the positive side of what we have in Christ, and raise the Christian up to the full height of his position. Ephesians has very decisive marks of the place it holds—the third place; for there is no book that so opens the heavenly places for us: Hebrews, indeed, as worshipers; but Ephesians, to set us there in Christ.

We have not the Christian as dead to sin or law or the world now, but first dead in sins, and then quickened and raised up with Christ, a wholly new creation. Sanctification is thus provided for: "We are His workmanship, created in Christ Jesus unto good works,

which God hath before ordained, that we should walk
in them."

Then we are "made to sit together in the heavenly
places in Christ Jesus."

And from being afar off are brought nigh to God,
and have access through one Spirit to the Father.

And not only so, but are made a spiritual habitation
of God, growing into a holy temple in the Lord.

Then we have the revelation by the Spirit of the
mystery of the Church before hid in God, that to the
principalities and powers in heavenly places might be
made known, through the Church, the manifold wisdom of God.

Then a prayer, that through the power of the Spirit
Christ may so dwell in the heart by faith that we may
be filled up unto all the fullness of God.

The Spirit, and union by the Spirit, with its result
the formation of the Church, as the body of Christ,--
these things, as is well known, characterize Fphesians.

And I might go on, but it needs not.   The place of
Ephesians as a third epistle is fully manifest, and this
is my object now.

4. *Colossians.*

Notice, again, how these epistles are connected together.   Romans and Galatians give the full clearance
of the believer from all that is against him,—sin, the
flesh, the world.   Romans introduces to Galatians by
"the old man crucified with Christ."   Galatians completes the deliverance.   Then Ephesians takes up the
positive side of quickening with Christ, the heavenly
place, and union by the Spirit.   This, by its "filled

with all the fullness of God," leads us to the central
truth in Colossians.

Colossians is a beautiful fourth epistle. It is not,
indeed, the path through the world itself, which, as I
have said, is never the *subject* of Paul's epistles, but it
is the *furnishing for* the path. Its characteristic text
is certainly chap. ii. 9, 10—" For in Him dwelleth all
the fullness of the Godhead bodily, and in Him ye are
filled up" (complete).

You will remember how we saw the division of 4
into 3 and 1. Notice, then, how these numbers characterize the text just mentioned. The two clauses are
stamped respectively with these two numbers: "In
Him dwelleth all the fullness of the Godhead "—3 ;
and "In Him ye are filled up [or complete]"—1.
For this is in fact our spiritual perfection, in which
true internal harmony is found.

And this is what the epistle as a whole develops. In
the first chapter is the first part, as indeed it is already
stated there : " For in Him all the fullness was pleased
to dwell "—so, manifestly, the Revised Version not-
withstanding, it should read. Then comes, in the
second and third chapters, the development of how in
this fullness we are filled up. And here the blessings
of Romans and Ephesians both are found, except the
being ourselves in heavenly places, because it is of life
down here the epistle speaks, yet the life of the risen
man to whom Christ is all, and his responsibility to
walk worthy of the Lord,—indeed to walk in Him.

²*Philemon.*

Philemon comes in here as a supplement, I doubt not.

I *was* a good while doubtful of its place, and yet once seen, it is simple enough. Onesimus is mentioned in Colossians, and was sent back at the very time of that letter, Philemon belonging himself to Colosse. It is strange, in fact, it should have been separated from that epistle, except from its being written to an individual, not an assembly as in the latter case.

The subject, too, no doubt seems different. It is nevertheless most beautifully connected as an appendix, as we shall easily see. For it is striking that addresses to masters and servants are found (along with other relations in life,) in both Ephesians and Colossians; to *masters* in Paul's epistles, *no where else;* thus this address to a master fittingly follows.

A reason, too, for these addresses in these two epistles is surely this, that the thought of the place in Christ, and the new life of which they speak, should not be taken enthusiastically to do away with the relationships of the present: a real danger, as it has proved, for some.

Now Philemon demonstrates practically how for the apostle these relationships remain. Onesimus is now by his conversion much "more than a servant, a brother beloved," yet Paul sends him back to his master, though he would gladly have retained him, but without *his* mind would do nothing. The epistle thus shows strikingly the true exalting power of Christianity, not intended to release from the duties or disadvantages of an earthly place,—*not* to be a lever to lift into earthly position or ease,—but to fill with a competency to serve in the lowest and lowliest, like Him whom we all serve.

How well Philemon fills its place here I need not, surely, point out.

5. *Philippians.*

And now Philippians, as an experimental close to this part, comes to tell us how great the gain for one to whom Christ is "all." The epistle is a blessed and wonderful Deuteronomy, in which sin is no longer before one, and the flesh can be dismissed as having no confidence in it. (This is the practical result of the lesson of Romans being learned.) It tells of one who has found the cross of Christ, the end of a path which leads out of the world to the highest place with God : and this is the moral lesson of Galatians. It speaks, too, of One in whom all is found for the heart—an Object outside the world, and above it: and this is Ephesians and Colossians. Finally, it tells us of the result as to all passed through here; of the competency of Christ so enjoyed for all exercises and all emergencies. A grand and triumphant conclusion to this first Pentateuch of Paul the apostle.

A glimpse at these things makes one long to pause and go more deeply into them. But this would be to give up what is before us at the present moment. We must even hasten on at an increased rate of progress.

The second Pentateuch of Paul commences with two epistles, the earliest of all he wrote :—

1. *The Epistles to the Thessalonians.*

The two epistles are alike addressed to the " church of the Thessalonians *in God the Father* and in the Lord Jesus Christ," and this is peculiar to them. It is significant therefore, of course, of the subject of the epistles, which are of great simplicity. The second is but an appendix to the first, upon a special subject.

The *first epistle*, written to those but recently converted, is full of the joy of the witness for Christ they were already giving, the work of their faith, the labor of their love, the patience of their hope in Christ; for young as that hope was yet, its endurance had been severely tested. All this manifested God's election of them, their reception into the family of God as begotten of the Spirit and Word, amid much affliction.

The rest of the epistle reminds them of what his own walk had been among them, speaks of his affection and anxiety for them, and, for their encouragement, communicates to them a new revelation from the Lord concerning the resurrection of the sleeping saints, to be caught up with the living when He comes. The last chapter exhorts them, as children of the day, not to be surprised in the night as others, to put on the breastplate of faith and love, and for a helmet the hope of salvation: the same Christian character as before dwelt upon; for what defense can there be against the world like the cultivating of the faith, love, and hope which are fixed beyond it?

The theme of the epistle, then, is the *family of God*, and their character, with which, not as something over and above, but as essential to its development, the doctrine of the Lord's coming is specially dwelt upon. It is referred to, indeed, again and again, all through, and the Thessalonians were converted to wait for God's Son from heaven.

The *second epistle* brings out even more, perhaps, the importance of this, speaking after John's manner to the babes of Antichrist, to be revealed before the *day of the Lord*—not His descent into the air,—should come. An apostasy from Christianity should precede and make way for the man of sin.

2. *The Epistles to the Corinthians.*

If the epistles to the Thessalonians give us the character and hopes of the children of God, those to the Corinthians speak of a fellowship in which the children of God are now gathered together. Corinthians gives us the Church of God, as the *practical fellowship of saints on earth*, not in the heavenly aspect in which Ephesians presents it. But upon earth there is a trinity of evil to oppose and corrupt, if possible, that which is of God; and Corinth was noted among the Greeks themselves for its vice and profligacy. The power of the Spirit of God had been shown signally here, and the Lord had much people in the city; but they had not maintained themselves in holy separateness from the evil around, and the epistle devoted to the order of the Church on earth is a striking witness to the incoming evils. Divisions had rent their fellowship, the wisdom of the world had displaced to a great extent the wisdom that was in Christ, the loose walk permitted among them outraged the very heathen, while from the idolatry around even they were not separate. Thus the world, the flesh, and the devil had place already in what was the temple of God on earth, and instead of mourning, they were rejoicing and puffed up.

The first division of the first epistle deals with these

evils; the second develops the internal order of the
Church: the subjection of the woman to the man, as
of the man to the Lord; the regulation of the Lord's
supper, the showing forth of His death; the gifts in
the body, and the spirit and manner of their exercise.
Subjection, testimony, mutual ministry in love,—these are
the things insisted on. The third division shows how
the Word of God itself, the fundamental doctrine of
the resurrection, was in question among them: the
whole basis of the assembly was being lost.

The *second* epistle is again an appendix to the first,
its subject being the ministry of the Word, its character as the ministry of the new covenant, its trials, exercises, sustaining power and compensations. Of this
the apostle is himself the living exponent, and all his
heart is told out in it; but we see also that ministry is
not confined to this public service, but that the ministering of one's goods even is also this.

3. *Hebrews.*

In the third place comes the epistle to the Hebrews,
which answers so clearly to the place it fills that few
words are needed to make this plain. It is largely a
commentary on a text in Leviticus, the " day of atone-
ment," only with the va:l of the sanctuary now rent,
and boldness to enter in through the blood of Jesus.
The priesthood of Christ is, of course, largely dwelt
on; and the going outside the camp, to which now the
Jewish Christians are urged, is the simple consequence
of the glory itself having for the third time left it, and
the sanctuary being now outside.

The epistle to the Hebrews finds thus its necessary

place among Paul's epistles, and there would be, if it were wanting, an evident and important gap ; while by itself, also, it could not stand. There is as little place for it elsewhere as here on the other hand it is clearly needed.

4. *The Epistles to Timothy.*

The epistles to Timothy speak of the Church as the house of God, to be ordered for Him in that holiness which becomes it. Therefore, in the first epistle, the provision of elders and deacons, the care for godliness and good doctrine every-where manifest. The Church of God is the pillar and ground of the truth, and we are to know how to behave ourselves in it.

But already there are teachers of the law, and blasphemers like Hymenæus and Alexander ; and the Spirit expressly assures us that in the latter times men shall apostatize from the faith, giving heed to seducing spirits and demon-teachings. The *second* epistle shows already a vast change. The house of God is become like a great house, with its gold and silver vessels indeed, but also those of wood and earth, and some to honor and some to dishonor. Now, therefore, one must purge one's self from these in order to be a vessel unto honor, and fellowship is to be maintained with those who call on the Lord out of a pure heart. The last days are more distinctly seen, and persecution ever for those who will live godly in Christ Jesus. The apostle's course is finishing with joy, and now we are commended to God and the word of His grace.

These are the wilderness books of the second series. How different from that bright Colossian epistle of the first ! And yet the soul of the apostle is bright. In

the removal of all that can be shaken, we learn but
the more what it is to have our portion in that which
cannot be shaken.

5. *Titus.*

Titus closes this series with the Deuteronomic assurance that God's way is holy as the end is sure. The
truth is according to godliness. The grace of God
which bringeth salvation teaches us that, denying
ungodliness and worldly lusts, we should live soberly,
righteously, and godly in this present world; looking
for that blessed hope, even the appearing of our great
God and Saviour, Jesus Christ, who gave Himself for
us, that He might redeem us from all iniquity, and
purify unto Himself a people for His own possession,
zealous of good works.

Thus fittingly Paul's epistles close. We have yet
before us the so-called Catholic Epistles, and the book
of Revelation.

The Catholic Epistles.

It is not, surely, without significance that there are just
eight writers of the New-Testament books; nor yet that
there are just *four* for the *seven* catholic epistles. They
have thus on the one side the numerical stamp of their
division; on the other, the seal of perfection on that
path through the world which they point out to us.
The number of their writers is that of their divisions
also, and they stand with the apostle of the circum-
cision first:—

1. Peter.
2. James.
3. John.
4. Jude.

1. *The Epistles of Peter.*

When Israel journeyed through the wilderness, of all the holy things carried by the Levites, the *ark went first.*

No wonder, for it was the throne of God, as we all know, and to put it there was just to proclaim the Master they served, and themselves before all things (if they acted in character with this,) an *obedient people.*

Now this is just the theme of the epistles of Peter. No doubt, in a sense, every book of Scripture, and not one alone, insists upon obedience; but with Peter it is here the theme, and it is a great one; for not all that seems even devotedness is this, still less that "obedience of Christ" to which he speaks of those he addresses as being "sanctified," *along with* "the sprinkling of blood;" so that the obedient ones are the blood-cleansed ones.

He speaks of them as elect, begotten to a living hope by Christ's resurrection, guarded through faith to salvation and an inheritance in heaven, their faith proved amid manifold trials ordained for praise at Christ's appearing. They are born again of the Word, children of obedience, redeemed with the precious blood of Christ, and calling on the Father, who judges according to every man's work. Thus they are started with the Word their sustenance, and the knowledge of the Lord's grace, to show forth His praises in a world which has rejected Him.

They are to be subject to authorities, fill the relationships of life aright, do well, suffer for it and take it patiently, and if for Christ's sake, rejoice. Judgment, too, begins here at the house of God.

This is the character of Peter's first Epistle. It is God on the throne, though a throne of grace, and the Father He who sits there; we His elect, begotten of His Word, are to walk in obedience.

The *second* epistle views not only the sin that is in the world, but in the Church also,—rebellion against all authority, that men may freely indulge their lusts. Here the cross and the glory characterize the path; the glory attracts us on, virtue (or courage) is what is needed by the way. We must add to faith virtue, and so ripen the fruit God looks for. Christ is coming, and the day of the Lord will be the destruction of ungodly men.

2. *James*.

James is the justification, not of the sinner by faith, as with Paul, but of the believer by his works; that is the justification of his faith itself,—not, therefore, before God, (who knows assuredly if it be real or not,) but before *men*. ": A man may say, Thou hast faith and I have works; *show me* thy faith without thy works;"—it is impossible,—"and I will *show thee* my faith *by* my works." Thus it is the fruits of *faith* which are alone in question, not simply morality; Abraham offering up his son, Rahab betraying her country, are not this: they are the witnesses of *faith*, and valuable as that; "faith, if *it* have not works, is dead, being alone."

The number of the epistle marks it thus as *testimony:* but testimony is toward man, not God. Abraham is justified by faith in Gen. xv., alone under the stars with God. But Abraham is justified by works when, long afterward, he offers Isaac up upon the altar. Then it is "ye *see* how faith wrought with his works."

The testing of this may seem at times minute. If you put the poor man in a poor place in your synagogue, how can you have recognized the glory of the *Lord* of glory? It is a question of faith, and where does faith see poverty or riches?

Another characteristic of James connected with this is *patience*. It is the fruit of faith distinctly, and what the trial of faith works. Therefore blessed is he who endureth trial. Only let patience have her perfect work, and you are perfect and entire, lacking in nothing. This too is covered by the number 2, which speaks of the low place before God,—not active obedience, but passive subjection.

Then the *Word* is what governs the soul. There is the mirror in which you are to see yourself. Your speech, too,—your own words—are a special test. Thus the general drift, and the details also, of James' epistle agree with its numerical place.

3. *The Epistles of John.*

John speaks of the *manifestation*, not of faith as such, but of that eternal life which, as *divine* life, produces in us the signs of our parentage. God is light and God is love: thus the life in us will display itself as love and righteousness. This is the general character of the first epistle.

But for this he introduces us first into the sanctuary where God is revealed,—not merely light, but " *in* the light." There the light must reveal us to ourselves, and the precious blood put away the sins revealed.

To be "in the light" becomes thus for John the definition of a Christian. The blood-cleansing does not extend beyond the limits of the light in which we are.

The *second epistle* connects the love and light together, emphasizing the side of light, or *truth*.

The *third epistle* connects them also, but emphasizing the *love*. Love to the brethren is in John a very special manifestation of "having passed from death unto life." The second epistle deals with the question of evil as against Christ—of antichristianity.

4. *Jude.*

Jude closes this series sadly with the warning of the departure of the Church from holiness and subjection to the Lord, so that at His appearing the ungodly ones long prophesied of as subjects of His judgment will be found within the Church itself. But the Lord will preserve His own, and mercy and peace be multiplied to them.

The Book of Revelation.

And now we come to Revelation, the one book of New-Testament prophecy, but which goes beyond the Old entirely. Notice, however, it is not in the New Testament a third division, but a fifth, and this for a very beautiful and obvious reason.

In the Old Testament, prophecy alone could lead the people of God into things which yet could not be proclaimed as present. A very characteristic text is, what the apostle quotes from Isaiah himself, "Eye hath not seen, nor ear heard, neither hath entered into the heart of man, the things which God hath prepared for them that love Him." But that is not now our condition, as the apostle's comment upon it shows: "But

God *hath* revealed them unto us by His Spirit; for the Spirit searcheth all things, yea, the deep things of God."

Most fittingly, therefore, do the epistles of Paul, in which the fullness of truth (see Col. i. 25) is given, take the place in the New Testament held by prophecy in the Old. But the place of Revelation is none the less a most blessed and significant one. It is a magnificent summing up—solemn, yet glorious,—of the divine ways with man; of the history of the Church and of the world alike; while beyond—as Israel from the plains of Moab could view their inheritance—our "foundation of peace," our Jerusalem, is shown to us, —her foundation in the displayed perfections of God Himself. Thus the *sevens* of the book, as I have already said, proclaim God's full accomplishment of all that has been in His heart so long. Here revelation closes, its volume is complete: what is beyond is sight, and the glory of God forever.

I have completed, then, for the present, my task. You must for yourselves, dear brethren, examine and judge if what I set myself to do, God's mercy has permitted me. For myself, it is evident that the numerical seal is on all Scripture, the witness of its completeness and of its perfect inspiration; but also a guide to the interpretation of the Word of a value possibly beyond all present thought. I trust that the Lord will permit me in His grace, if He tarry yet, to show you something that I have seen of this. But the book itself is before us all. It needs and invites the research of all. It is this that the slight outline I have given may, I trust, be used for. If God has been at pains to write

His Word after this manner, it is that we may profit by it. If He has given us here a new field of labor, rich with the most wonderful possibilities, shall we or shall we not avail ourselves of it? Who will go into the Lord's harvest-field?—Who? And may indeed the harvest be of joy and praise and abundant blessing, for Christ's sake.